Air Fryer Toaster Oven Cookbook for Beginners

350 Crunchy, Fast and Delicious Recipes from The Air Toaster Oven for Beginners with a Great Passion for Cooking

BY

JESSICA WILLIAMS

2

By reading this document, the reader agrees that under no circumstances is the author responsible for any losses, direct or indirect, which are incurred as a result of the use of information contained within this document, including, but not limited to, — errors, omissions, or inaccuracies.

Table of Contents

CHAPTER ONE

INTRODUCTION

Air fryers work by coursing every tourist around the food and needn't bother with fat or oil. You can add an incredibly modest amount to improve the taste if you wish, simultaneously, this normally only a teaspoon full. This suggests that they are ideal for anyone and everyone who acknowledges delectable sound nourishment. They are particularly significant for the people who are checking the calories. Consuming fewer calories and calorie tallying can regularly be testing and frequently precludes any fried food, just by the nature in which they are cooked. Air fryers are not only for chips! Any kind of food, from chicken pieces to pineapple rings, can be cooked right now. The main restricting element is your creative mind.

An air fryer is a conservative, ledge machine that utilizations convection warming to course air around your food. The food is held inside in a container, and a fan quickly moves air around the food, encompassing it likewise to food submerged in hot oil in a profound fryer. At last, it functions admirably to give food that firm, seared surface without a great deal of extra fat. Air fryers utilize next to zero oil to get a similar impact as customary profound broiling.

They guarantee no awful, searing scents in the house. They are functional and simple to clean and make an incredible expansion to any kitchen. This is a more seasoned adaptation of the air fryer, yet on a basic level, the cooking technique is the equivalent. The fryer has been out for a while and has an awesome name. One principle distinction between the two is that the actifry includes a moving oar inside the unit to keep food turning and uniformly cooked. There are advan. It's a thought that must interest sharp cooks all over the place - profound broiling without the trouble and threat of huge volumes of hot oil, to avoid anything related to the wellbeing dangers.

The fryer works by planning a warmed stream of air over and around the nourishment, which is contained in a box. The holder is held in a bureau which openings into the front of the mechanical assembly - so no all the more bringing down of nourishment into the hot oil. You set the cooking temperature with a clear indoor controller, and the time with a turning clock. The fryer turns itself off close to the end. To plan more than one nourishment thing, basically use the bushel divider. All the normal fried nourishments can be cooked with remarkable accomplishment. For sure, even cakes and brownies can be cooked in the Airfryer - not things that you would want to cook in a fryer! This underlines the flexibility of the machine. It's extremely like a convection oven, set up with a bushel to allow it to manage nourishments that would customarily go into the significant fryer.

Regardless, it's presumably steady with express that chips (or fries if you're in the US!) will be the nourishment of most energy to most buyers. Here the Airfryer is as a general rule particularly incredible. Because you put aside a bit of exertion to ask about the best way to deal with using the machine - the best sort of potatoes to use, the particular cooking time, and so on, you'll be more than content with the results. It justifies reviewing that you do truly need to use a pinch of oil - you'll need to incorporate around an enormous segment of a tablespoon of oil each time. The cooking time frame is around five minutes upon sums and complexities well and significant singing or oven warming.

It consumes minimal more space than a typically estimated food processor and looks noteworthy and modern. Since all the parts that contact the food are dishwasher-safe, it's anything but difficult to keep clean. It accompanies a speedy beginning manual for make you go, just as a far-reaching formula book with 30 distinct plans for you to attempt - as alluded to prior, you may be astonished at the scope of sudden foods that you can cook in the Airfryer. The Airfryer certainly proceeds as it should. The advantages to the soundness of using less fat in cooking can not be generally be denied. This fryer can help to accomplish that - and produce incredible tasting food also.

The thing I find commonly shocking about Airfryer is the way that it plans southern style nourishment without using any oil. I have to surrender, and I am fairly a French fry somebody who is dependent and am really envisioning having the choice to set up a bunch of uniquely designed fries rapidly without using oil. I am moreover envisioning the way that these fries will contain 80% less fat than those that I generally cook in the significant fryer or buy from pass through joints. There are a huge amount of various things that can be cooked in the Airfryer that are unfathomable moreover.

Blessed the s Airfryer will in like manner cook chicken without using any oil. That infers I can eat all the fried chicken I need and not have to worry over all the fat that I, for the most part, gain

13

from the oil in the chicken. In like manner, the chicken will be crunchy anyway clammy and fragile inside.

Stuffed vegetables are something different that can be cooked in the Airfryer. Many persons are not quite a bit of a stuffed vegetable fan, but rather I understand there are many individuals out there who love them. If you are one of them, at that point, this is something to anticipate for you. Cooking stuffed veggies has never been simpler than it is with the Rapid Air Technology that s utilizes in the Airfryer.

The vast majority may be astounded by this next sort of food that can be cooked in the s Airfryer. After dinner has been readied utilizing this advanced profound fryer sweet can likewise be set up in it. The truth is out; all the brownies, biscuits, and cake you need to eat for pastry can be cooked right now. They end up extraordinary.

There are a ton of focal points and advantages that can be picked up by utilizing the s Airfryer to cook foods without utilizing any oil. Regardless of whether you are somebody who needs to eat more beneficial, needs to get in shape, or who simply needs to eat some home-prepared food, this is the main profound fryer required in your kitchen. There are a ton of incredible highlights that accompany it and a ton of extraordinary adornments that it utilizes. Yet, the most significant thing to remember is that it doesn't utilize oil for cooking foods.

Get thinner Eating Fried Foods.

Can we think it was conceivable to get thinner eating fried foods? Indeed, years back, individuals were able to add fried foods to their eating routine and shed pounds doing it. Presently don't misunderstand me fried foods are as yet stuffing. However, the Airfryer will take 80% of the fat that is in those southern style foods that we as a whole love such a great amount out. There are a few incredible advantages and highlights this new cooking innovation will have the option to give any individual who cherishes fried foods and needs to get more fit.

How the Airfryer works is by utilizing protected Rapid Air Technology to prepare fried food. The air is pushed around in the bin at a high pace and permits the food to be cooked at temperatures of up to 200 degrees Celsius (392 degrees Fahrenheit).

Foods that are cooked in oil are typically oily and slick inside, which makes them taste clammy to many individuals. In the Airfryer, the same sort of dampness will be available; however, there won't be any oily tastes metal impacts to stress over.

There are a variety of kinds of foods that individuals typically eat when they are attempting to get more fit. The majority of these foods have no taste and are not ones that many individuals like. Imagine a scenario where you could eat natively constructed French fries or fried potato chips as a piece of your eating regimen. Would that help you to remain progressively dedicated?

The explanation that many individuals don't lose the weight that they are attempting to lose is because they can't adhere to the eating routine arrangement that they have picked. Individuals tend to need to get themselves some kind of sweet or fried food when they have arrived at a weight reduction objective that they have been attempting to accomplish for some time.

With the Airfryer, those treats can be ones that are beneficial for you. You may be devouring 20% of the fat that you would ordinarily expand when you eat the foods that the Airfryer cooks. At that point, this is the one bit of cooking gear that you need to have. There are a ton of other incredible things about it that you will need to think about if you are keen on getting in shape by eating fried foods.

Low Fat Air Fryer Cooking Chips

Presumably, the principal reason that numerous individuals consider purchasing a low-fat air fryer, for example, the Tefal Actifry or the Air Fryer, is just because they can set up those much dearest southern style chips yet with next to no or no oil. This makes these machines engaging if you are attempting to get thinner! In any case, there are at any rate two things that prevent individuals from making that buy; can you just cook chips, and do they genuinely possess a flavor like the broiled ones you truly love? In a nutshell, both the two specific machines referenced course tourist around the food that regularly prepares the food much quicker than other ordinary strategies. Notwithstanding, the Tefal utilizes an oar that pushes and turns the food inside the skillet. Interestingly, the s doesn't do this, so on account of specific foods, you should shake the dish part of the way through the cooking procedure.

In answer to the main inquiry, truly, you can cook significantly more than contributes your air fryer. Moreover, exactly what you can get ready will rely upon the specific model as a result of contrasts in the manner these machines work. For Tefal, you will have to do nothing until the machine 'pings' when the food is prepared. In this, you frequently need to give the crate a shake part of the way through the cooking procedure relying upon what you are cooking—coming back to the nature of the chips. You will locate that both the above models will deliver fundamentally the same as the final result. They are not equal to the broiled assortment. Saying this does not imply they don't look and taste great as they positively do. In any case, a great many people report that they are the nearest thing to the first that you can get and far better than low-fat oven chips.

Even though you can likewise utilize solidified chips to set them up crisp, you should simply chip your potatoes as ordinary. Slight French fries are the quickest to cook and just take nit more than 12 minutes. You can absorb the chips water for thirty minutes to expel the greater part of the starch, dry them all together and shower over half to one tablespoon of oil. Warmth the fryer for two or three minutes and fly in the chips.

The essential contrast with the s is that it has a crate, a food divider, and a cooking compartment. This implies it is most likely progressively adaptable for the kitchen. You can prepare brownies and coat the potatoes that you couldn't do in the Tefal. Conversely, it would be progressively hard to make curries (however not feasible) in the s where the Tefal makes it extremely simple. This is only a fast outline of air fryers, which has inferred that cooking contributes a low-fat air fryer doesn't create chips that taste precisely like southern style ones. It suggests anyway that they are likely the nearest you can create and are a lot more beneficial.

The truth is out, and the Airfryer cooks fried foods without utilizing oil. I don't think about you, yet I love eating fried foods. What we can't care for is the undesirable outcomes that I get, for example, weight increase, stomach related issues, and the oil that comes overflowing out of my pores. I figure everybody ought to have the option to eat fries, chicken, and other fried foods without stressing over managing the entirety of the medical problems. So, which is the reason they have turned out with such a cutting edge development in cooking innovation? There are a couple of features that the Airfryer has that makes it worth owning.

One remarkable thing about this front line significant fryer is that it cooks singed nourishments without using oil. That suggests there is 80% less fat in the sum of the nourishments that you cook in it. That infers there is no convincing motivation to worry over gaining weight or driving a heartbreaking lifestyle, and it will fit in with an eating routine you may be on. There are furthermore a couple of phenomenal additional items that go with the Airfryer that make it top of the line.

One is the food separator that permits you to cook a couple of various foods one after another. The separator keeps the foods separate from one another, so there is no compelling reason to stress over one kind of food having an aftertaste like another. Darn, I am truly going to miss my fries having an aftertaste like chicken!

Another incredible embellishment is the creative air channel that accompanies it. The air channel will sift through the entirety of the fumes that normally top off your whole house when you are cooking something in oil. This implies you don't need to stress over your kitchen or some other territory possessing a scent like cooking oil or fried foods for a considerable length of time after you cook. Likewise, if you are a bustling guardian or somebody who should have the option to perform various tasks, there is a clock that can be set for as long as 30 minutes. When the food is prepared and prepared to eat, the clock will go off, and a "prepared" ready will sound telling you that the time has come to eat. This is a helpful frill that everybody could utilize a greater amount of nowadays.

This Airfryer is an unquestionable requirement that has a profound fryer for any individual who needs to have the option to eat more beneficial and all the more helpfully. If you are burnt out on searing your foods in oil and managing the entirety of the delayed consequences as am I, at that point, you need to look at this thing. You will have the option to sear foods without utilizing any cooking oil and eat them with 80% less fat. You will likewise have the option to utilize the entirety of the frill that accompany it to make your life simpler.

This Is What an Air Fryer Does to Your Food

The air fryer furor is clearing the country, yet what is an air fryer? Is it extremely worth your well-deserved money? This helpful apparatus professes to mirror the consequences of profound singing with simply tourists and a small measure of oil. The air fryer is an amped-up ledge convection oven. Its conservative space encourages considerably quicker cooking. The highest point of the unit holds a warming component and a fan. Sightseeing rushes down and around food put in a fryer-style bushel. This fast flow makes the food fresh, much like profound broiling. Cleanup is excessively simple, as well, and most units have dishwasher-safe parts.

What would you be able to make in it?

Air fryers make a phenomenal showing concocting solidified foods that are intended to taste rotisserie—think solidified french fries, chicken wings, and mozzarella sticks. They additionally work superbly with comparative recipes produced using scratch. Perhaps the best part is that air fryers can prepare, as well.

How can it work?

The air fryer is an amped-up ledge convection oven. Its smaller space encourages considerably quicker cooking. The highest point of the unit holds a warming component and a fan. Tourists rush down and around food set in a fryer-style bushel. This quick course makes the food fresh, much like profound singing.

Different interesting points.

• Cost. On the expensive side of home machines, air fryers run somewhere in the range of $100 and $300, relying upon size and highlights. Locate the best air fryer for your way of life.

• Space. Greater than a toaster, the air fryer is not a little apparatus. You'll have to surrender important capacity (or counter) space to house one.

• Skills. Air fryers are fitting and play. Spot your food in the crate, set the time, and the temperature and bam! You're cooking.

• Taste and surface. Air fryers will give you results a lot nearer to profound fricasseeing than your oven will, toward the day's end, it's as yet not the equivalent.

• Healthier? The contention can be made that it produces more beneficial food by utilizing less oil. Solidified french fries arranged in the air fryer contain somewhere in the range of 4 and

6 grams of fat versus their pan-fried partner at an incredible 17 grams for every serving.

Toward the day's end, this is an entirely smooth device. At the point when you're concocting things like french fries or chicken tenders, you can't beat it. The outcomes are far superior to oven broiling, and your kitchen remains cool. While it works admirably cooking different meats and vegetables, the air fryer truly sparkles at mock profound singing. So if you don't regularly eat southern-style foods, it's most likely not worth the venture.

Warmth Wave

Would it be that makes air fryers novel? The appropriate response may be, "Nothing, truly." Air fryers are convection ovens in a container, implying that like a customary oven, they have a warming component. Like a somewhat fancier oven with a convection highlight, they have a fan that courses the tourist, keeping the temperature reliable all through the cooking zone. On account of quicker than-a-typical oven heat move abilities from that quickly circling air, convection ovens can abbreviate the cooking time of certain foods, conceivably giving them a crispier outside that brand-cognizant marketers appear to consider to be like fried food.

Preposterous

Another prescribed formula was an entire chicken like the one found on the front of the formula booklets. Having now utilized the machine, I had some genuine geometry questions, most altogether how to pack an entire feathered creature into the air fryer's container.

Apologies, Please Fry Again

So here's the arrangement: you needn't bother with one of these things. They're boisterous, even the enormous ones have a shockingly little limit, they don't show improvement over an oven, and you presumably have an oven in any case. They'd likewise require knocking your toaster and coffeemaker onto a capacity rack.

Rather, in case you're into the air-fricasseeing thought, spare the conceivably critical measure of cash you'd spend on one (very good quality models can cost $400 or more) and move up to a convection highlight whenever your genuine oven croaks.

The advertising materials for the scores of organizations that make these sight-seeing blowers will reveal to you that they are an extraordinary method to cook that eliminates fat. Yet, great master, fried will be fried, and "air-fried" isn't that. Better to eat well more often than not, then go to your preferred fried chicken spot on your birthday, or do it up at home with several liters of canola oil and a Dutch oven. The uncommon portion of flawlessness is better than the reliable trickle of remarkableness.

The Best Air Fryer Toaster Ovens

At ordinary interims, there is a mechanical kitchen assembly that begins a delicate fever in our stomachs. Two or three years back, it was the Instant Pot—which was, in a general sense, a rebranded pressure cooker. By and by, the hot thing in the air fryer.

While air fryers do offer an essentially less messy, less slick way to deal with singe nourishment, they generally stay single. People starting now have such an enormous number of machines in our kitchens for what it's worth. Luckily, makers saw this reality and immediately united the air fryer with toaster ovens. The subsequent combo—the air fryer toaster oven—is the zenith in brisk and productive food arrangement.

What's more, the mix of the two capacities is great. Here's a gadget that permits you to air fry your food, however, toast it, heat it, dry out it, cook it, and—now and again—rotisserie it. If you are the sort of individual who prepares food in the microwave, at that point, this thing isn't for you.

Be that as it may, if you like to prepare your food, so it holds its flavor profile without radiation. At that point, here are the absolute best air fryer toaster ovens available.

Deco Chef XL

If you have somewhat chicken just relaxing around keeping down to be changed into a delicious new chicken, by then, the 12 quart Deco Chef XL oven is for you. Alongside the rotisserie work, it can air fry, get dried out and sear. The Deco Chef XL has a standard convection oven worked in, and all the plate you'll need to warm that meat. It's even got two immense handles for controlling the time and warmth. Quick and dirty here, this contraption is all limited.

Best Choice Products

Practically identical in structure to the Deco Chef XL, the Best Choice Products 11.5 quart 8-in-1 XL channel the handles for mechanized gets. It has an OK huge window so you can sit in the kitchen and watch all of the three cooking racks get dried out a pound of pineapple. The air fryer oven has about eight presets for cooking, or you can go freestyle and do it without anybody's assistance.

Soing Air Fryer Oven XL

The Soing Air Fryer Oven XL may appear as though a Star Wars junk can droid, yet it is a great deal more—it can flame broil, toast, fry, prepare, cook, warm, and dry out. The oven has the 8-in-1 assignment too, which implies fewer kitchen machines to stop up the counter. There's very little you can't fit right now, you are arranging cooking an entire pig. In which case, you are treating it terribly.

Cuisinart TOA-60

Cuisinart is one of the most confided in brands in kitchen apparatuses, and the Cuisinart TOA-60 proceeds with that inheritance. With a fairly minimized impression, this air fryer toaster oven trenches the computerized for an exemplary four-handle format. It heats, sears and toasts and obviously, air fries. You probably won't have the option to fit a whole chicken in there. However, you can, at any rate, cautiously warm the parts you didn't complete the previous evening.

Black+Decker

As its name suggests, the Black + Decker TO3265XSSD Extra Wide Crisp 'N Bake is, well, extra wide. This considers more bread, a whole close to home pizza, and the capacity to prepare without warming up the kitchen with your standard oven. It wouldn't be on this rundown if it couldn't afford air fry likewise, and at this value point (under $80), it's a generally excellent arrangement for an across the board kitchen apparatus. Also, it's at a bargain at present.

Emeril Lagasse Power Air Fryer

Emeril Lagasse may be off TV for the occasion. However, his eponymous product offerings are as yet kicking it up a score. To keep the plays on words rolling, the Emeril Lagasse Power Air Fryer will bam you in the face with its snappy cook innovation.

This is a 1500-watt ledge oven, which means it gives a great deal of warmth in a little space. With the goal, that score is kicked up in any event one. Additionally, most convection ovens just have only three warming components, and this one has five. Air fry, prepare, rotisserie, get dried out, toast, warm, cook, sear, slow cook, and warm your approach to culinary expert quality dinners. Or, on the other hand, heat that whole pack of Bagel Bites. Your call. Additionally, it's 22% off for Amazon Prime Members at this moment.

NuWave Bravo XL

While the greater part of these multifunction ovens has comparable highlights, the NuWave Bravo XL has one that the others don't—a connected computerized temperature test that will naturally close down the oven when your meat (or chicken or fish) has arrived at the proper temperature. With one-contact cooking and 12 presets, the NuWave Bravo XL is a strong air fryer toaster oven. On the entirety of that, it's discounted for 29% off.

CHAPTER TWO

BREAKFAST RECIPES

Air-Fried Cinnamon and Sugar Doughnuts

Ingredients

• 41 m

• 9 servings

- 276 cals

Ingredients

- 1/2 cup white sugar

- 2 1/2 tablespoons margarine, at room temperature

- 2 enormous egg yolks

- 2 1/4 cups universally handy flour

- 1 1/2 teaspoons heating powder

- 1 teaspoon salt

- 1/2 cup acrid cream

- 1/3 cup white sugar

- 1 teaspoon cinnamon

- 2 tablespoons margarine, liquefied, or varying

- Add all ingredients to list

Directions

• Prep; 25 m

• Cook16 m

• Ready In; 41 m

1. Press 1/2 cup white sugar and margarine together in a bowl until brittle. Include egg yolks and mix until very much consolidated.

2. Sift flour, heating powder, and salt into a different bowl. Spot 1/3 of the flour blend and 1/2 the acrid cream into the sugar-egg blend; mix until consolidated. Blend in the rest of the flour and acrid cream. Refrigerate mixture until prepared to utilize.

3. Mix 1/2 cup of sugar and then cinnamon together in a bowl.

4. Roll batter out onto a delicately floured work surface to 1/2-inch thick. Cut nine enormous circles in the batter; cut a little hover out of the focal point of every huge hover to make donut shapes.

5. Slightly heat an air fryer to 340 degrees F.

6. Brush 1/2 of the dissolved spread over the two sides of the doughnuts.

7. Place 1/2 doughnuts into the bushel of the air fryer; cook for 8 minutes. Paint cooked doughnuts with the staying liquefied spread and promptly plunged into the cinnamon-sugar blend. Rehash with the rest of the doughnuts.

Cook time may differ by the quality and limit of your air fryer; check and modify likewise.

Nourishment

260 calories; 42.5 g starches; 9.5 g fat; 4.3 g protein; 66 mg cholesterol; 397 mg sodium.

Air Fryer Breakfast Frittata

Ingredient

• 1/4 pound breakfast sausage, completely cooked and disintegrated

• 4 eggs, daintily beaten

- 1/2 cup destroyed Cheddar-Monterey Jack cheddar mix

- 2 tablespoons red chime pepper, diced

- 1 green onion, cleaved

- 1 squeeze cayenne pepper (discretionary)

- Cooking splash

Direction

- Prep; 15 m

- Cook; 20 m

- Ready In; 35 m

1. Combine meat, eggs, Cheddar-Monterey Jack cheddar, chime pepper. Onion, and cayenne in a bowl and blend to consolidate.

2. Slightly heat the air fryer to about 360 degrees F. Splash a nonstick 6x2-inch cake dish with cooking shower.

3. Place egg blend in the readied cake container.

4. Cook until the frittata is set.

Nourishment

370 calories; 2.9 g starches; 31.2 g protein; 27.4 g fat; 443 mg cholesterol; 694 mg sodium.

Air Fryer Sweet Potato Hash

Ingredient

• 2 huge sweet potato, cut into little 3D squares

• 2 cuts bacon, cut into little pieces

• 2 tablespoons olive oil

• 1 tablespoon smoked paprika

• 1 teaspoon ocean salt

• 1 teaspoon ground dark pepper

• 1 teaspoon dried dill weed

• Add all ingredients to list

Directions

1. Slightly heat an air fryer to 400 degrees F (200 degrees C).

2. Toss sweet potato, bacon, olive oil, paprika, salt, pepper, and dill in a huge bowl. Spot blend into the Slightly heat used air fryer. Cook for 12 to 16 minutes. Check and mix the following 10 minutes and afterward like clockwork until firm and caramelized.

Nourishment

195 calories; 31.4 g starches; 3.7 g protein; 6 g fat; 3 mg cholesterol; 447 mg sodium.

Tex-Mex Air Fryer Hash Browns

Ingredient

• 1 1/2 pounds potatoes, stripped and cut into 1-inch 3D shapes

- 1 tablespoon olive oil

- 1 red chile pepper, seeded and cut into 1-inch pieces

- 1 little onion, and then cut them into 1-inch pieces

- 1 jalapeno and then cut into 1-inch rings

- 1/2 teaspoon of olive oil

- 1/2 teaspoon taco flavoring blend

- 1/2 teaspoon ground cumin

- 1 squeeze salt and ground dark pepper to taste

Directions

1. Soak the potatoes in cool water for about 20 minutes.

2. Slightly heat the air fryer to about 320 degrees F. Channel the potatoes, dry them with a spotless towel, and move to an enormous bowl. Shower 1 tablespoon olive oil over the potatoes and hurl to cover. Add them to the Slightly heat used air fryer bin. Set the clock for 18 minutes.

3. Put ringer pepper, onion, and jalapeno in the bowl recently utilized for potatoes. Sprinkle in 1/3 teaspoon of olive oil, taco flavoring, ground cumin, salt, and pepper. Hurl to cover.

4. Transfer the potatoes from the air fryer into the bowl with the vegetable blend. Return the unfilled container to the air fryer and raise the temperature to 356 degrees F.

5. Quickly hurl the substance of the bowl to blend the potatoes equitably with the vegetables and flavoring. Move blend into the container. Cook for 6 minutes, shake the crate, and keep cooking until potatoes are sautéed and firm, around about five minutes more. Serve right away.

Make sure to utilize new potatoes as old ones don't fresh well.

Don't leave any of the seeds in the peppers. They will consume and detonate. If you need more warmth, include additional jalapenos or utilize a spicier pepper like serrano or habanero.

Nourishment

Per Serving: 189 calories; 6.3 g fat; 34.7 g starches; 4 g protein; 0 mg cholesterol; 79 mg sodium.

Simple Air Fryer French Toast Sticks

Ingredient

• 4 cuts somewhat stale thick bread, for example, Texas toast

• Material paper

• 2 eggs, delicately beaten

• 1/4 cup milk

• 1 teaspoon vanilla concentrate

• 1 teaspoon cinnamon

• 1 squeeze ground nutmeg (discretionary)

Directions

1. Cut each cut of bread into thirds to make sticks. Cut a bit of material paper to fit the base of the air fryer bushel.

2. Slightly heat air fryer to about 340 degrees F.

3. Stir together eggs, milk, vanilla concentrate, cinnamon, and nutmeg in a bowl until all-around joined. Dunk each bit of bread into the egg blend, ensuring each piece is very much submerged. Shake each breadstick to evacuate abundance fluid and spot in a solitary layer in the air fryer craze. Cook in bunches, if important, to abstain from congestion the fryer.

4. Cook for about five minutes and then turn the bread pieces, and cook for an extra five minutes.

Nourishment

Per Serving: 235 calories; 8.4 g fat; 29.6 g starches; 11.2 g protein; 188 mg cholesterol; 423 mg sodium.

Air Fryer Sausage Patties

Ingredient

• 1 (12 ounces) bundle hotdog patties, (for example, Johnsonville®)

• 1 serving non-stick cooking splash

Direction

1. Slightly heat an air fryer to 400 degrees F (200 degrees C).

2. Place hotdog patties into the container in 1 layer, working in clusters if fundamental.

3. Cook Slightly in the air fryer for about five minutes. Haul the crate out, turn frankfurter over, and cook until a moment read thermometer embedded into the focal point of a patty peruses 160 degrees F (70 degrees C), around 3 minutes more.

Nourishment

145 calories; 0.7 g sugars; 14.1 g protein; 9 g fat; 46 mg cholesterol; 393 mg sodium.

Air-Fried Cinnamon and Sugar Doughnuts

Ingredient

• 1/2 cup white sugar

- 2 1/2 tablespoons margarine, at room temperature

- 2 enormous egg yolks

- 2 1/4 cups universally handy flour

- 1/2 teaspoons heating powder

- 1 teaspoon salt

- 1/2 cup harsh cream

- 1/3 cup white sugar

- 1 teaspoon cinnamon

- 2 tablespoons margarine, dissolved or varying

Direction

1. Press 1/2 cup white sugar and margarine together in a bowl until brittle. Include egg yolks and mix until all-around joined.

2. Sift flour, heating powder, and salt into a different bowl. Spot 1/3 of the flour blend and 1/2 the sharp cream into the sugar-egg

blend; mix until joined. Blend in the rest of the flour and acrid cream. Refrigerate batter until prepared to utilize.

3. Mix 1/2 cup of sugar and the cinnamon together in a bowl.

4. Roll mixture out onto a daintily floured work surface to 1/2-inch thick. Cut nine huge circles in the batter; cut a little hover out of the focal point of every huge hover to make donut shapes.

5. Slightly heat an air fryer to about 340 degrees F.

6. Brush 1/2 of the softened spread over the two sides of the doughnuts.

7. Place 1/2 doughnuts into the crate of the air fryer; cook for 8 minutes. Paint cooked doughnuts with the staying dissolved margarine and quickly dunk into the cinnamon-sugar blend. Rehash with the rest of the doughnuts.

Cook time may fluctuate by the quality and limit of your air fryer; check and change as needs are.

Nourishment

9.7 g fat; 43.5 g starches; 4.3 g protein; 66 mg cholesterol; 390 mg sodium.

Air Fryer Breakfast Toad-in-the-Hole Tarts

Ingredient

• 1 sheet solidified puff cake, defrosted

• 4 tablespoons destroyed cheddar

• 4 tablespoons diced cooked ham

• 4 eggs

• hacked new chives (discretionary)

Direction

1. Slightly heat the air fryer to 400 degrees F (200 degrees C).

2. Unfold cake sheet on a level surface and cut into 4 squares.

3. Place 2 cake squares in the air fryer bushel and cook 6 to 8 minutes.

4. Remove crate from air fryer. Utilize a metal tablespoon to press each square tenderly to shape space. Spot 1 tablespoon of cheddar and 1 tablespoon ham in each opening and pour 1 egg on each.

5. Return crate to air fryer. Cook to wanted doneness, around 6 minutes more. Expel tarts from the bushel and let cool about five minutes. Rehash with outstanding cake squares, cheddar, ham, and eggs.

6. Garnish tarts with chives.

The secure approach to get your egg in the gap is to break it into a little squeeze glass first and afterward empty it into the gap.

Nourishment

Per Serving: 446 calories; 31 g fat; 27.9 g sugars; 14.2 g protein; 199 mg cholesterol; 377 mg sodium.

Air Fryer Churros

Ingredient

- 1/4 cup margarine

- 1/2 cup milk

- 1 squeeze salt

- 1/2 cup universally handy flour

- 2 eggs

- 1/4 cup white sugar

- 1/2 teaspoon ground cinnamon

Direction

1. Melt margarine in a pan over medium-high warmth. Pour in milk and include salt. Lower warmth to medium and heat to the point of boiling, ceaselessly blending with a wooden spoon. Rapidly include flour at the same time. Continue mixing until the batter meets up.

2. Remove from warmth and let cool for 5 to 7 minutes. Blend in eggs with the wooden spoon until choux baked well meets up. Spoon mixture into a baked good sack fitted with a huge star tip— Channel mixture into strips straight into the air fryer bin.

3. Air fry churros at 340 degrees F (175 degrees C) for about five minutes.

4. Meanwhile, consolidate sugar and cinnamon in a little bowl and pour it onto a shallow plate.

5. Remove fried churros from the air fryer and move in the cinnamon-sugar blend.

Nourishment

Per Serving: 172 calories; 9.8 g fat; 17.5 g starches; 3.9 g protein; 84 mg cholesterol; 112 mg sodium.

Air Fryer Bacon

Ingredient

• 1/2 (16 ounces) bundle bacon

1. Slightly heat an air fryer to 390 degrees F (200 degrees C).

2. Lay bacon on a solitary layer inside the air fryer crate; it's alright if there is some covering or collapsing.

3. Cook for about eight minutes and then flip the bacon and cook until bacon is fresh, around 7 minutes more.

4. Transfer cooked bacon to a plate fixed with paper towels to absorb overabundance oil.

Nourishment

Per Serving: 173 calories; 17 g fat; 0.2 g starches; 4.4 g protein; 26 mg cholesterol; 315 mg sodium.

Air Fryer Apple Fritters

• Cooking splash

• 1 cup generally useful flour

• 1/4 cup white sugar

• 1/4 cup milk

• 1 egg

- 1/2 teaspoons preparing powder

- 1 squeeze salt

- 2 tablespoons white sugar

- 1/2 teaspoon ground cinnamon

- 1 apple - stripped, cored, and hacked

- Glaze:

- 1/2 cup confectioners' sugar

- 1 tablespoon milk

- 1/2 teaspoon caramel concentrate, (for example, Watkins™)

- 1/4 teaspoon ground cinnamon

Direction

1. Slightly heat an air fryer to about 340 degrees F . Spot a material paper round into the base of the air fryer—splash with nonstick cooking shower.

2. Mix flour 1/3 cup egg, sugar, milk, preparing powder, and salt together in a little bowl. Mix until joined.

3. Mix two tablespoons of sugar with the cinnamon in a bowl and then sprinkle over apples until covered. Blend apples into the flour blend until consolidated.

4. Drop squanders utilizing a treat scoop onto the base of the air fryer bin.

5. Air-fry in the Slightly heated fryer for about five minutes. Flip squanders and cooks until brilliant, around about five minutes more.

6. In the interim, blend confectioners' sugar, milk, caramel concentrate, and cinnamon in a bowl. Move wastes to a cooling rack and sprinkle with the coat.

Nourishment

290 calories; 64.9 g starches; 5.5 g protein; 2.1 g fat; 48 mg cholesterol; 248 mg sodium.

Air Fryer Baked Apple

Your preferred grain or custom made apple granola on the planet couldn't beat this incredibly hot, wickedly scrumptious Air Fryer Baked Apple.

This formula turns crude, healthy ingredients into something unrecognizable in an ideal manner conceivable. Air fryers are a blessing from above making sugary, caramelized, and mellowed treats feasible, regardless of what your weight reduction objective.

All you need is only a smidge of margarine and cinnamon. This Baked Apple (or pear!) formula is an American most loved sure to bring solace your way without busting the calorie bank. Indeed, Air Fryer Baked Apples check in at less than 150 calories (with starches of the SmartCarb assortment), however, bring the pastry shop taste of a portion of your preferred calorie-loaded baked goods. Presently how would you like dem apples? Bend over for a flex nibble.

Ingredients:

• 1 medium apple or pear

• 2 Tbsp. hacked pecans

- 2 Tbsp. raisins

- 1 ½ tsp. light margarine, dissolved

- ¼ tsp. cinnamon

- ¼ tsp. nutmeg

- ¼ cup of water

Directions:

1. Slightly heat air fryer to 350° F.

2. Cut the apple or pear down the middle around the center and spoon out a portion of the tissue.

3. Place the apple or pear in griddle (which might be furnished with the air fryer) or on the base of the air fryer (in the wake of evacuating the extra).

4. In a little bowl, consolidate margarine, cinnamon, nutmeg, pecans, and raisins.

5. Spoon this blend into the focuses of the apple/pear parts.

6. Pour water into the container.

7. Bake for 20 minutes.

Cinnamon Rolls

Ingredients

• 1 pound solidified bread mixture, defrosted

• ¼ cup margarine softened and cooled

• ¾ cup dark colored sugar

• 1½ tablespoons ground cinnamon,

Cream Cheese Glaze

• 4 ounces cream cheddar, mellowed

• 2 tablespoons margarine, mellowed

• 1¼ cups powdered sugar

• ½ teaspoon vanilla

Instructions

1. Let the bread mixture come to room temperature on the counter. On a gently floured surface, fold the mixture into a 13-inch by 11-inch square shape. Position the square shape, so the 13-inch side is confronting you. Brush the dissolved margarine everywhere throughout the batter, leaving a 1-inch fringe revealed along the edge most distant away from you.

2. Combine the dark-colored sugar and cinnamon in a little bowl. Sprinkle the blend equitably over the buttered batter, keeping the 1-inch outskirt revealed. Fold the mixture into a log beginning with the edge nearest to you. Roll the batter firmly, making a point to move equally and push out any air pockets. When you find a workable pace edge of the mixture, press the batter onto the move to seal it together.

3. Cut the sign into eight pieces, cutting gradually with a sawing movement, so you don't level the mixture. Turn the cuts on their sides and spread with a perfect kitchen towel. Let the rolls sit in the hottest piece of your kitchen for 1½ to 2 hours to rise.

4. To make the coating, place the cream cheddar and margarine in a microwave-safe bowl. Mellow the blend in the microwave for 30 seconds one after another until it is anything but difficult to mix. Bit by bit includes the powdered sugar and mix to join. Include the vanilla concentrate and race until smooth. Put in a safe spot.

5. When the rolls have risen, pre-heat the air fryer to 350°F.

6. Transfer 4 of the moves to the air fryer bushel. Air-fry for about five minutes. Turn the turns over and air-fry for an additional 4 minutes. Rehash with the staying four rolls.

7. Let the moves cool for several minutes before coating. Spread enormous dabs of cream cheddar coat on the warm cinnamon rolls, permitting a portion of the coating to trickle down the side of the rolls. Serve warm and appreciate it!

Gluten-Free Cranberry Pecan Muffins

Cranberries are in many heated things throughout the fall and winter months. We make cranberry sauce for Thanksgiving and proceed through Christmas with a lot more plans to which we include cranberries.

We don't need to confine preparing with cranberries just to fall and winter months. Treats and biscuits with crisp cranberries can be for whenever of the year. You can generally get a solidified sack of cranberries when new cranberries are out of season.

To be straightforward, I've just utilized crisp cranberries a couple of times as of recently. I've bounced into the cranberry marsh this year and made a few biscuits and a snappy bread with new cranberries.

Truly, they were powerful. The cranberries heated flawlessly, including a delectable pungency. If you have to loosen up toward the evening, make some tea and appreciate this gluten-free cranberry walnut biscuits air fryer formula.

Biscuits are delicious for breakfast whenever of the year. This being a blender formula causes this a formula you to can prepare in a matter of seconds by any means. So we should get preparing!

Ingredients

• 1/4 cup cashew milk (or utilize any dairy or non-dairy milk you like)

• 2 enormous eggs

- 1/2 tsp. vanilla concentrate

- 1 1/2 cups Almond Flour

- 1/4 cup Monkfruit (or utilize your favored sugar)

- 1 tsp. preparing powder

- 1/4 tsp. cinnamon

- 1/8 tsp. salt

- 1/2 cup new cranberries

- 1/4 cup hacked walnuts

Instructions

1. Add to blender container the milk, eggs, and vanilla concentrate and mix 20-30 seconds.

2. Add in the almond flour, sugar, preparing powder, cinnamon, and salt – mix another 30-45 seconds until very much mixed.

3. Removed the blender container from the base and mix in the 1/2 of the new cranberries and the walnuts. Add the blend to silicone biscuit cups. Top every one of the biscuits with the rest of crisp cranberries.

4. Place the biscuits into the air fryer container and prepare on 325 for 12-1about five minutes – or until toothpick tells the truth.

5. Remove from air fryer and cool on wire rack.

6. Drizzle with a maple coat whenever wanted. I likewise showered liquefied white chocolate over a portion of the biscuits.

Notes

For Oven Baking, heat in a Slightly heat the 325-degree oven for 25 to 30 minutes, or until a toothpick tells the truth.

Nutty spread and Jelly Air Fried Doughnuts

Doughnuts:

• 1 1/4 Cups universally handy flour

- 1/3 cup sugar

- 1/2 Teaspoon heating powder

- 1/2 Teaspoon heating pop

- 3/4 teaspoon salt

- 1 Egg

- 1/2 cup buttermilk

- 1 Teaspoon vanilla

- 2 Tablespoons unsalted margarine, liquefied and cooled

- 1 Tablespoon softened spread for brushing the tops

Filling:

- 1/2 Cup Blueberry or strawberry jam (not jam)

Coating:

- 1/2 cup powdered sugar

• 2 Tablespoons milk

• 2 Tablespoons nutty spread

• Pinch of ocean salt

Instructions

Whisk together the flour, sugar, heating powder, preparing pop and salt.

Beat together the eggs, softened margarine, buttermilk, and vanilla.

Make a well in the focal point of the dry ingredients and pour in the wet. Utilize a fork to join and afterward complete the process of blending with a huge spoon, just until the flour is fused.

Turn the mixture in a round, floured surface. Note that it will be clingy from the outset. Work the batter somewhat until it meets up and afterward pat it out to a 3/4" thickness.

Utilizing a 3 1/2" shaper, cut out mixture adjusts and brush with the dissolved spread. Cut out 2" bits of material paper (shouldn't be precise) and place every mixture around on the paper, at that point into the air fryer. Work in clumps relying upon what number of will fit in your fryer.

Fry at 350 degrees for 11 minutes. Fill every donut with jam utilizing a crushed container or baked good pack.

Whisk together the coating ingredients and sprinkle over every donut.

Air Fryer French Toast Soldiers

Ingredients

• Philips Airfryer

• 4 Slices Wholemeal Bread

• 2 Large Eggs

• ¼ Cup Whole Milk

• ¼ Cup Brown Sugar

• 1 Tbsp Honey

• 1 Tsp Cinnamon

• Pinch of Nutmeg

• Pinch of Icing Sugar

Instructions

1. Chop up your cuts of bread into troopers. Each cut should make four warriors.

2. Place the remainder of your ingredients (aside from the icing sugar) into a blending bowl and blend well.

3. Dip each fighter into the blend, so it is all around covered and afterward place it into the Air Fryer. At the point when you're set, you will have 16 warriors and afterward, should all be decent and wet from the blend.

4. Place on 160c for 10 minutes or until they are decent and fresh like toast and are never again wet. Part of the way through cooking turn them over with the goal that the two sides of the fighters have a decent opportunity to be uniformly cooked.

5. You can serve alongside a sprinkle of icing sugar and some new berries.

Notes

I locate that like when you make breadcrumbs, and this formula works best on bread that has gone somewhat stale. Nutrition esteems our best gauge dependent on the product we use at Recipe this and are implied as a guide. If you depend on them for your eating regimen, utilize your favored sustenance number cruncher.

Air Fryer Frittata

Air fryers make for a flawlessly light approach to appreciate the entirety of the flavor of your fried, oily top choices in a thinned down manner, and this Air Fryer Frittata is a prime (pardon the play on words) "eggs-sufficient."

Rather than staring off into space about the "eternity prohibited" early lunch foods, the entirety of your companions are getting a charge out of, create a light, protein-stuffed and flavorful feast that will dispatch your day in the correct direction. Mushrooms, tomato, and chive draw out the serious weapons for a garden new flavor to supplement feathery billows of egg white that needs no help from cheddar. Try not to trust us? Give it a shot because there's nothing to lose here... aside from creeps from your abdomen.

Ingredients:

• 1 cup egg whites

• 2 Tbsp. skim milk

• ¼ cup cut tomato

• ¼ cup cut mushrooms

• 2 Tbsp. hacked crisp chives

• Black pepper, to taste

Directions:

1. Slightly heat Air Fryer at 320° F.

2. In a bowl, consolidate all the ingredients.

3. Transfer to a lubed skillet (which might be given the air fryer) or to the base of the air fryer (after expelling the frill)

4. Bake for 1about five minutes or until frittata is cooked through.

Breakfast Puffed Egg Tarts

Breakfast Puffed Egg Tarts are ideal for any event. Not exclusively would they be able to amuse your visitors this current Mother's Day informal breakfast yet, also can make the most stunning nibble on your next game night?

Since you know how adaptable these egg tarts are, you should make some at this point. Are you a game?

Slightly heat air fryer to 390°F (200°C)

Ingredients

Universally handy flour

One sheet solidified puff baked good (a large portion of a 17.3-oz/490 g bundle), defrosted

¾ cup destroyed cheddar, (for example, Gruyère, Cheddar or Monterey Jack), separated

Four enormous eggs

1 tbsp minced crisp parsley or chives

1. On a softly floured surface, unfurl cake sheet. Cut into four squares.

2. Place two squares in the air fryer container, dividing them separated. Air-fry for 10 minutes or until cake is light brilliant dark-colored.

3. Open container and, utilizing a metal spoon, push down the focuses of each square to make a space. Sprinkle 3 tbsp (45 mL) cheddar into every space and cautiously break an egg into the focal point of every cake.

4. Air fry for about 12 mins or until eggs are cooked to wanted consistency. Move to a wire rack set over waxed paper and let cool for about five minutes. Sprinkle with a large portion of the parsley, whenever wanted. Serve warm.

5. Repeat stages 2 to 4 with the rest of the baked good squares, cheddar, eggs, and parsley.

Tips to Make Egg Tarts

The sheet of puff baked good 9 inches (23 cm) square for this formula. If your sheets are an alternate size, or the cake arrives in a square, fold or trim it into a 9-inch (23 cm) square as vital.

Air fryers become hot, particularly when warmed to most extreme temperatures. Use oven cushions or gloves when contacting the apparatus and when opening and shutting the bin.

To make including the egg simpler, break the egg into a little cup before sliding it onto the puff baked good.

Breakfast Puffed Egg Tarts

Slightly heat air fryer to 390°F (200°C)

Ingredients

• All-reason flour

• 1 sheet solidified puff baked good a large portion of a 17.3-oz/490 g bundle, defrosted

• 3 /4 cup destroyed cheddar, for example, Gruyère, Cheddar or Monterey Jack, partitioned

• 4 enormous eggs

• 1 tbsp minced crisp parsley or chives discretionary

Instructions

1. On a softly floured surface, unfurl baked good sheet. Cut into 4 squares.

2. Place 2 squares in the air fryer container, dispersing them separated. Air-fry for 10 minutes or until baked well is light brilliant dark-colored.

3. Open container and, utilizing a metal spoon, push down the focuses of each square to make a space. Sprinkle 3 tbsp (45 mL) cheddar into every space and cautiously split an egg into the focal point of every baked good.

4. Air fry for about 12 minutes or until eggs are cooked to wanted doneness. Move to a wire rack set over waxed paper and let cool

for about five minutes. Sprinkle with a large portion of the parsley, whenever wanted. Serve warm.

5. Repeat stages 2 to 4 with the rest of the baked good squares, cheddar, eggs, and parsley.

The sheet of puff baked goods ought to be around 9 inches (23 cm) square for this formula. If your sheets are an alternate size, or the cake arrives in a square, fold or trim it into a 9-inch (23 cm) square as fundamental. Air fryers become extremely hot, particularly when warmed to most extreme temperatures. Use oven cushions or gloves when contacting the machine and when opening and shutting the crate. To make including the egg simpler, split the egg into a little cup before sliding it onto the puff cake.

Air Fryer-Perfectly Done, Heavenly French Toast

Ingredients

• 4 cups of bread

• 2 eggs

- ⅔ cup of milk

- 1 teaspoon of vanilla

- 1 tablespoon of cinnamon

Instructions

1. In a little bowl, combine the eggs, milk, cinnamon, and vanilla. At that point, beat until the eggs are separated, and everything is blended well.

2. Then dunk each bit of bread into the blend and afterward shake to get the abundance off, as you do, put them into your readied skillet

3. Airfryer for about five minutes at 320 degrees F. At that point, flip them over and do an additional 3 minutes.

4. Serve with maple syrup and appreciate it!

CHAPTER THREE

LUNCH RECIPES

Air fryer stacked heated potatoes.

Solace food just got snappier and simpler civility of your air fryer. These fresh potatoes may appear to be liberal, yet keen bits of bacon, cheddar, and harsh cream include large flavor while holding calories and sat fat under control. The mystery is the middle cut bacon—it concocts pleasant and firm, and yields

71

simply enough container drippings to make these potatoes truly sparkle. Serve these delicate fresh spuds with a skillet-burned steak and a side of your preferred steamed veggies for a fast and simple dinner.

Ingredients

• 11 ounces infant Yukon Gold potatoes (around 8 [2-inch] potatoes)

• 1 teaspoon olive oil two focus cut bacon cuts 1

• 1/2 tablespoons cleaved crisp chives

• 1/2 ounce finely destroyed decreased fat cheddar (around 2 Tbsp.)

• 2 tablespoons decreased fat harsh cream 1/8 teaspoon fit salt

Direction

1. Toss potatoes with oil to cover. Spot potatoes in air fryer crate, and cook at 350°F until fork delicate, 2about five minutes, and blending potatoes once in a while.

2. Cook bacon on medium until firm, around 7 minutes. Expel bacon from skillet; disintegrate—spot potatoes on a serving platter; gently squash potatoes to part. Sprinkle with bacon drippings. Top with chives, cheddar, harsh cream, salt, and disintegrated bacon.

Air Fryer Potato Chips

The firm, crunchy, and addictive, air fryer potato chips have 60 percent less fat than their locally acquired partners. Indeed, making potato contributes your air fryer requires a smidgen of exertion—however, the outcome is a salty tidbit that is, in reality, truly sound. Shows improvement over that?

Acing air fryer potato chips takes practice—and you'll need to mind the part of the way through cooking, at that point all the more now and again towards the finish of their cooking cycle. Use tongs to painstakingly isolate any chips that have adhered to one another to guarantee they cook equally, and expel any chips that are completely crisped.

Ingredients

- 1 medium Russet potato, unpeeled, cut into 1/8 inch thick cuts (around 3/4 pound)

- 1 tablespoon canola oil

- 1/4 teaspoon ocean salt

- 1/4 teaspoon newly ground dark pepper

- Canola oil

- 1 teaspoon hacked new rosemary

Dietary Information

- Calories 100

- Fat 3.5g

- Sat fat 0g

- Unsatfat 3.2g

- Protein 2g

- Carbohydrate 15g

- Fiber 1g

- Sugars 1g

- Added sugars 0g

- Sodium 140mg

- Calcium 0% DV

- Potassium 8% DV

Direction

1. In a huge bowl of cold water, splash potato cuts for 20 minutes. Channel potatoes; pat dry with paper towels.

2. Wipe bowl dry; at that point, including oil, salt, and pepper. Include potatoes; hurl delicately to cover.

Carne Asada Steak Sandwiches

Chipotle chile powder has a smoky, natural profile and isn't as hot as ground red pepper. These incredible steak sandwiches receive the reward of the chipotle chile powder and are overflowing with the season.

Ingredients

• 12 ounces flank steak, cut

• 1 1/2 teaspoons olive oil

• 1 teaspoon ground cumin

• 3/4 teaspoon chipotle chile powder

• 1/4 teaspoon fit salt

• 1/4 cup canola mayonnaise

• 2 tablespoons slashed crisp cilantro

• 1/2 teaspoon ground lime skin

• 1 tablespoon crisp lime juice

• 1 minced garlic clove

- 1 (12-ounce) entire grain French bread roll, split longwise

- Cooking shower

- 1/2 ready avocado, meagerly cut

- 8 (1/8-inch-thick) tomato cuts

- 1 jalapeno pepper, meagerly cut

Nourishing Information

- Calories 416

- Fat 16g

- Sat fat 3.6g

- Monofat 9.1g

- Poly fat 2.2g

- Protein 24g

- Carbohydrate 46g

• Fiber 3g

• Cholesterol 38mg

• Iron 4mg

• Sodium 754mg

• Calcium 19mg

• Sugars 2g

Est. included sugars 1g

Direction

1. Slightly heat flame broil to medium-high warmth.

2. Brush steak with oil; sprinkle uniformly with cumin, Chile powder, and salt. Let stand 1about five minutes.

3. Combine mayonnaise, cilantro, skin, juice, and garlic in a bowl; refrigerate.

4. Hollow out top and base parts of bread, leaving a 1/2-inch-thick shell; save torn bread for another utilization. Coat cut sides of bread with cooking shower. Spot roll parts, chop sides down, on barbecue rack; flame broil 1 moment or until toasted. Expel from flame broil—coat flame broil rack with cooking shower. Add steak to barbecue; flame broils 10 minutes or until the wanted level of doneness, turning periodically. Spot steak on a cutting board; let stand about five minutes—Cutover the grain into slender cuts.

5. Spread a top portion of bread with mayonnaise blend. Mastermind avocado over a base portion of bread; top with steak, tomato, jalapeño, and top portion of bread. Cut the sandwich into four pieces.

Faultless Paleo Pumpkin Muffins

Ingredients

• Philips Airfryer

• 1 Cup Pumpkin Puree

• 2 Cups Gluten-Free Oats

- ½ Cup Honey

- 2 Medium Eggs beat

- 1 Tsp Coconut Butter

- 1 Tbsp Cocoa Nibs

- 1 Tbsp Vanilla Essence

- 1 Tsp Nutmeg

Instructions

1. Place every one of your ingredients in the blender and mix until smooth.

2. Place the biscuit blend into little biscuit cases, spreading it out more than 12 separate ones.

3. Place in the Air Fryer and cook for 1about five minutes on 180c.

4. Serve when cool.

Notes

If you favor, you can make it all the more chocolatey by including some cocoa powder and some messed up bits of dull chocolate. However, I incline toward it like the formula above.

Nourishment

Calories: 121kcal | Carbohydrates: 22g | Protein: 3g | Fat: 2g | Saturated Fat: 0g | Cholesterol: 27mg | Sodium: 13mg | Potassium: 108mg | Fiber: 2g | Sugar: 12g | Vitamin A: 3215IU | Vitamin C: 0.9mg | Calcium: 17mg | Iron: 1mg

Note: Nutrition esteems our best gauge dependent on the product we used. This is implied as a guide. If you depend on them for your eating routine, utilize your favored nourishment adding machine.

Blueberry Lemon Muffin

Blueberry Lemon Muffin Air Fryer Recipe a simple to make biscuit for breakfast or early lunch, Mother's Day, Father's Day. The biscuits can likewise be oven prepared at 350 degrees for 12-1about five minutes.

- Prep Time: 5-8 min.

- Cook Time: 10-12 min.

- Total Time: 25-35 min.

- Yield: 1 oz.

- Category: Breakfast

- Cuisine: American

Ingredients

- 2 1/2 cups self-rising flour

- 1/2 cup Monk Fruit (or utilize your favored sugar)

- 1/2 cup of cream

- 1/3 cup of avocado oil (any light cooking oil)

- 3 eggs

- 1 cup blueberries

- Zest in 1 lemon

- Juice in 1 lemon

- 1 tsp. vanilla

- Brown sugar for fixing (a touch of sprinkling on every biscuit, not exactly a teaspoon)

Instructions

1. In a little bowl, combine oneself with rising flour and sugar. Put in a safe spot.

2. In a medium bowl, consolidate cream, oil, lemon juice, eggs, and vanilla.

3. Add flour blend with the fluid blend and then mix just until mixed. Mix in the blueberries.

4. Spoon the player into silicone cupcake holders, sprinkle ½ tsp—dark colored sugar on every biscuit.

5. Bake at about 330 degrees for eight minutes, check biscuits at 6 minutes to guarantee they are not cooking excessively quickly. Put a toothpick into the focal point of the biscuit, and when the

toothpick tells the truth and the biscuits have cooked, they are finished. No compelling reason to over-heat the biscuits, they will keep on cooking for one more moment or two after they are expelled from the air fryer.

6. Remove and cool.

Notes

This formula can likewise be oven heated at 350 degrees for 12-1about five minutes.

Paleo Pumpkin Muffins

Ingredients

• Philips Airfryer

• 1 Cup Pumpkin Puree

• 2 Cups Gluten-Free Oats

• ½ Cup Honey

- 2 Medium Eggs beat

- 1 Tsp Coconut Butter

- 1 Tbsp Cocoa Nibs

- 1 Tbsp Vanilla Essence

- 1 Tsp Nutmeg

Instructions

1. Place every one of your ingredients in the blender and mix until smooth.

2. Place the biscuit blend into little biscuit cases, spreading it out more than 12 separate ones.

3. Place in the Air Fryer and cook for 1about five minutes on 180c.

4. Serve when cool.

Notes

If you lean toward, you can make it all the more chocolatey by including some cocoa powder and some messed up bits of dull chocolate, yet I favor it like the formula above.

Nourishment

Calories: 121kcal | Carbohydrates: 22g | Protein: 3g | Fat: 2g | Saturated Fat: 0g | Cholesterol: 27mg | Sodium: 13mg | Potassium: 108mg | Fiber: 2g | Sugar: 12g | Vitamin A: 3215IU | Vitamin C: 0.9mg | Calcium: 17mg | Iron: 1mg

Nourishment Infoplease Note: Nutrition esteems our best gauge dependent on the product we used. If you depend on them for your eating routine, utilize your favored nourishment adding machine.

Hash Brown

Ingredients

• Large potatoes - 4 - stripped and finely ground.

• Corn flour - 2 tablespoon

• Salt - to taste

• Pepper powder - to taste

• Chili chips - 2 teaspoon

• Garlic powder - 1 teaspoon (discretionary)

• Onion Powder - 1 teaspoon (discretionary)

• Vegetable Oil - 1 + 1 teaspoon

Instructions

1. Soak the destroyed potatoes in chilly water. Channel the water. Rehash the progression to empty overabundance starch of potatoes.

2. In a non-stick container heat, 1 teaspoon of vegetable oil and saute destroyed potatoes till cooked marginally for 3-4 mins.

3. Cool it down and move the potatoes to a plate.

4. Add cornflour, salt, pepper, garlic, and onion powder and bean stew drops and combine generally.

5. Spread over the plate and pat it immovably with your fingers.

6. Refrigerate it for 20 minutes

7. Slightly heat air fryer at 180C

8. Take out the now refrigerated potato and gap into equivalent pieces with a blade

9. Brush the wire container of the air fryer with little oil

10. Place the hash darker pieces in the bin and fry for 1about five minutes at 180C

11. Take out the container and flip the hash tans at 6 minutes with the goal that they are air-fried consistently

12. Serve it hot with ketchup

Air Fryer Bacon

Ingredients

• 6 pieces of bacon

Nourishment

• Serving Size: 1 cut

• Calories: 37

• Sugar:1

• Saturated Fat: 2.8

• Carbohydrates:1

• Fiber: 0

Instructions

1. Place the bacon in the base of your air fryer bushel if you have a 3.5-quart air fryer and had the option to get six pieces of bacon on the base. Spot the wire rack over your bacon that accompanied the air fryer. This is discretionary.

2. Cook and then open up the air fryer and flip the bacon. Put the air fryer bin back in and cook for an additional 3 minutes or until anyway firm you like your bacon.

Air Fryer Omelet

Ingredients

• 2 eggs

• 1/4 cup milk

• Pinch of salt

• Fresh meat and veggies, diced (I utilized red ringer pepper, green onions, ham, and mushrooms)

• 1 teaspoon McCormick Good Morning Breakfast Seasoning – Garden Herb

• 1/4 cup destroyed cheddar (I utilized cheddar and mozzarella)

Instructions

1. In a little bowl, blend the eggs and milk until very much consolidated.

2. Add a spot of salt to the egg blend.

3. Add your veggies to the egg blend.

4. Pour the egg blend into a very much lube 6″x3″ container.

5. Place the container into the crate of the air fryer.

6. Cook at 350° Fahrenheit for 8-10 minutes.

7. Halfway through preparing to sprinkle the breakfast flavoring onto the eggs and sprinkle the cheddar over the top.

8. Use a slender spatula to relax the omelet from the sides of the skillet and move to a plate.

9. Garnish with additional green onions, discretionary

Fast Air Fryer Breakfast Pockets

Ingredients

• One box puff baked good sheets.

• 5 eggs

- 1/2 cup meat disintegrates, cooked

- 1/2 cup bacon, cooked

- 1/2 cup cheddar, destroyed

Instructions

1. Cook eggs as ordinary fried eggs. Add meat to the egg blend while you cook, whenever wanted.

2. Spread out puff baked good sheets on a removing board and cut square shapes with a cut-out or blade, ensuring they are generally uniform so they will fit pleasantly together.

3. Spoon favored egg, meat, and cheddar combos onto half of the baked good square shapes.

4. Place a baked good square shape on the blend and press edges together with a fork to seal.

5. Spray with shower oil if you wanted a sparkly, smooth cake, yet it truly is discretionary.

6. Place breakfast pockets in the air fryer bushel and cook for 8-10 minutes at 370 degrees.

7. Watch cautiously and check every 2-3 minutes for wanted done-ness.

Spanish Frittata

Ingredients

To fit a little dish or the Phillips Air Fryer container.

· 3 large unfenced eggs

· ½ chorizo hotdog – cut

· 1 major potato – standard bubbled and cubed

· ½ cup solidified corn

· olive oil

· hacked herbs of your decision – I utilized parsley

· ½ wheel of feta

· salt/pepper

Direction

1. Pour a decent glug of olive oil in the dish of the Air Fryer (or your skillet on the stove), and include the chorizo, corn and the potato.

2. Set the Air Fryer on 180C and cook the hotdog and potato until marginally seared.

3. Break the 3 eggs into a little bowl and beat with a fork—season with salt and pepper.

4. Pour eggs over the potato and hotdog in the dish and top with crumbled feta and slashed parsley.

5. Cook for an additional about five minutes, check and, if necessary, cook for one more moment or something like that.

6. When cooked, turn out on a plate and present with stout tomato relish and some new rocket.

Slightly heat the oven to 180C and afterward cook the potato and meat in an oven-verification dish on the stovetop. At the point when the potato has sautéed marginally, beat the eggs in a little astound and pour the potato and hotdog. Top with feta and parsley and prepare in the oven until the eggs are set.

Airfryer French Toast Sticks

Ingredients

- 4 pieces bread (whatever sort and thickness wanted)

- 2 Tbsp spread (or margarine, mellowed)

- 2 eggs (delicately beaten)

- 1 squeeze salt

- 1 squeeze cinnamon

- 1 squeeze nutmeg

- 1 squeeze ground cloves

• 1 tsp icing sugar (or potentially maple syrup for topping and serving)

Nourishment

Calories: 178kcal

Fat: 15g

Soaked fat: 8g

Cholesterol: 194mg

Sodium: 193mg

Potassium: 60mg

Starches: 2g

Sugar: 1g

Protein: 5g

Nutrient A: 590%

Calcium: 25%

Iron: 0.8%

Instructions

1. Sligtly heat up Airfryer to 180* Celsius.

2. In a bowl, tenderly beat together two eggs, a sprinkle of salt, a couple of substantial shakes of cinnamon, and little portions of both nutmeg and ground cloves.

3. Butter the two sides of bread cuts and cut into strips.

4. Dredge each strip in the egg blend and organize it in Airfryer (you should cook in two groups).

5. After 2 minutes of cooking, delay the Airfryer, take out the dish, ensuring you place the container on a warm, safe surface, and splash the bread with cooking shower.

6. Once you have liberally covered the strips, flip and shower the subsequent side too.

7. Return skillet to the fryer and cook for four additional minutes, checking following a few minutes to guarantee they are cooking equitably and not consuming.

8. When the egg is cooked, and bread is brilliant darker, expel from Airfryer and serve right away.

9. To enhancement and serve, sprinkle with icing sugar, top with whip cream, shower with maple syrup, or present with a little bowl of syrup for plunging.

Mozzarella, Ham, and Basil Panini

Serve these basic squeezed sandwiches with a pickle and some vegetable chips.

Ingredients

• 1 (16-ounce) portion crusty bread, cut down the middle on a level plane

• Four teaspoons of Dijon mustard and four teaspoons balsamic vinegar

• 1 1/4 cups meagerly cut new mozzarella cheddar

• 12 basil leaves 8 ounces cut 33%-less-sodium cooked store ham, (for example, Healthy Choice)

• Two improved hot cherry peppers,

• sliced one huge plum tomato, daintily cut Cooking shower

Wholesome Information

• Calories 371

• Calories from Fat 30%

• Fat 12.5g

• Sat fat 6.1g

• Monofat 5g

• Poly fat 0.6g

• Protein 20.2g

• Carbohydrate 44.9g

• Fiber 1.8g

- Cholesterol 46mg

- Iron 3mg

- Sodium 976mg

- Calcium 220mg

Direction

1. Brush cut side of the base bread half with mustard; brush the cut side of the top half with vinegar. Top base half with mozzarella, basil, ham, peppers, and tomato. Top with outstanding bread half.

2. Heat a huge nonstick skillet over medium warmth—coat skillet with cooking splash. Add sandwich to the dish; top with another overwhelming skillet—Cook for about five minutes on each side or until brilliant. Cut the sandwich into six wedges.

Turkey Reuben Panini

Ingredients

- 8 (1/2-ounce) cuts flimsy cut rye bread

- 1/4 cup sans fat Thousand Island dressing

- 8 (1/2-ounce) flimsy cuts decreased fat Swiss cheddar

- 1/4 cup refrigerated sauerkraut, flushed and depleted

- 8 ounces store, low-sodium turkey bosom, (for example, Boar's Head)

Wholesome Information

- Calories 268

- Fat 7.5g

- Sat fat 3g

- Monofat 0.6g

- Poly fat 0.4g

- Protein 25.2g

- Carbohydrate 25.7g

- Fiber 3.1g

- Cholesterol 35mg

- Iron 1.7mg

- Sodium 819mg

- Calcium 304mg

Direction

1. Spread one side of each bread cut equitably with 1/2 teaspoons dressing.

2. Place one cheddar cut on the dressed side of every one of four bread cuts; top each with one tablespoon sauerkraut and 2 ounces turkey.

3. Top each sandwich with one cheddar cut and one bread cut, Coat on the outside of the sandwich with cooking shower.

4. Heat an enormous skillet over medium-high warmth. Add sandwiches to skillet.

5. Place a cast-iron or other substantial skillet on sandwiches; press delicately to smooth sandwiches (leave cast-iron skillet on sandwiches while they cook).

6. Cook for about three minutes until cooked and cheddar dissolves.

Excursion Perfect Lobster Rolls

Ingredients

• 1/3 cup cleaved celery

• 1/2 teaspoon ground lemon skin

• Two tablespoons cleaved green onions

• 1 tablespoon finely cleaved new tarragon

• 3 tablespoons canola mayonnaise

• 1 1/2 tablespoons crisp lemon juice

- 1/2 teaspoon Dijon mustard

- 1/4 teaspoon legitimate salt

- 1/4 teaspoon dark pepper

- 1/8 teaspoon ground red pepper

- 3/4 pound lobster meat, steamed and hacked

- 4 (1/2-ounce) New England-style sausage buns, toasted

Healthful Information

- Calories 284

- Fat 10.3g

- Sat fat 0.8g

- Monofat 4.9g

- Poly fat 2.7g

- Protein 21.7g

- Carbohydrate 22.4g

- Fiber 0.3g

- Cholesterol 65mg

- Iron 1.5mg

- Sodium 731mg

- Calcium 61mg

Direction

1. Combine initial 11 ingredients in a huge bowl, blending admirably; spread and chill in any event 60 minutes.

2. Divide lobster blend equally among buns.

Chicken Parmesan Burgers

Ingredients

- 2 (3-ounce) square crusty bread rolls

- 1 garlic clove, split

- 1/2 pound ground chicken

- 1/3 cup in addition to 2 tablespoons lower-sodium marinara sauce, separated

- 1/2 teaspoon hacked crisp rosemary

- 1/2 teaspoon hacked crisp thyme

- 1/4 teaspoon squashed red pepper

- 1/8 teaspoon legitimate salt

- 1/8 teaspoon dark pepper

- Cooking splash

- 1/4 cup destroyed part-skim mozzarella cheddar, separated

- 8 basil leaves

Dietary Information

- Calories 427

- Fat 14.4g

- Sat fat 4.5g

- Monofat 5.3g

- Poly fat 2.3g

- Protein 28.9g

- Carbohydrate 55.4g

- Fiber 1.2g

- Cholesterol 83mg

- Iron 2.9mg

- Sodium 742mg

- Calcium 112mg

Direction

1. Slightly heat the oven.

2. Cut moves down the middle. Spot bread, cut side up, on a heating sheet. Cook for 3 minutes or until gently sautéed. Expel bread from the dish. Rub each cut with the cut side of garlic. Put in a safe spot.

CHAPTER FOUR

DINNER RECIPES

Air Fryer French Fries

Air fryer French fries are the ideal method to make fries at home, and my family cherishes these!

Ingredients

• 3 medium potatoes (I am utilizing chestnut)

• 1/4 teaspoon garlic powder/granulated garlic

• Salt and pepper to taste

• 1 1/2 tablespoons oil of decision (I love utilizing avocado oil since it has a high smoke point. Coconut likewise functions admirably.)

Instructions

1. Wash your potatoes, and pat them dry. I don't strip mine, however, don't hesitate to do that.

2. Slice your potatoes to the size fries you need, and attempt to be fairly steady with the size to take into account in any event, cooking. (Note: bigger fries may require marginally more cook time.)

3. Toss your fries with the oil, garlic, salt, and pepper. You can hurl them in a bowl, or hurl them in your air fryer crate if you are lethargic like me! 😆 🍟

4. Cook them on 400 in the air fryer for around 20 minutes (more for bigger, steak fries), and hurl them around two or multiple times during the cooking to help equally cook.

5. If you need to make them look extravagant, sprinkle some slashed new parsley on top. Truly, I simply did this for the photos. We never include parsley, in actuality.

Notes

Nourishment data is estimated and was determined to utilize a formula sustenance name generator.

Air Fryer French Fries

Sum Per Serving

Calories 278 Calories from Fat 90

% Daily Value*

Fat 10g15%

Soaked Fat 1g6%

Sodium 31mg1%

Potassium 1319mg38%

Starches 39g13%

Fiber 7g29%

Protein 8g16%

Nutrient C 36.4mg44%

Calcium 96mg10%

Iron 10.4mg

Coconut Shrimp and Spicy Marmalade Sauce

Ingredients

• 8 huge shrimp shelled and deveined

• 8 ounces of coconut milk

- 1/2 cup destroyed improved coconut

- 1/2 cup panko bread

- 1/2 teaspoon cayenne pepper

- 1/4 teaspoon legitimate salt

- 1/4 teaspoon new ground pepper

- 1/2 cup orange jelly

- 1 tablespoon nectar

- 1 teaspoon mustard

1/4 teaspoon hot sauce

Instructions

1. Clean the shrimp and put it in a safe spot.

2. In a little bowl, whisk the coconut milk and season with salt and pepper. Put in a safe spot. In a different little bowl, whisk together the coconut, panko, cayenne pepper, salt, and pepper.

3. One at once, plunge the shrimp in the coconut milk, the panko, and afterward place in the bin of the fryer. Rehash until all the shrimp are covered. Cook the shrimp for about twenty minutes at 350 degrees or until the shrimp are cooked through.

4. Whisk together the preserves, nectar, mustard, and hot sauce.

5. Serve the shrimp with the sauce right away.

Sustenance Facts

Potassium 348mg10%

Sugars 76g25%

Fiber 1g4%

Sugar 57g63%

Protein 15g30%

Nutrient A 445IU9%

Nutrient C 5.9mg7%

Calcium 254mg25%

Iron 5.2mg29%

Coconut Shrimp (An AirFryer Review)

Sustenance Fact

Calories 623 Calories from Fat 279

% Daily Value

Fat 31g48%

Immersed Fat 25g156%

Cholesterol 82mg27%

Sodium 864mg38%

Potassium 348mg10%

Sugars 76g25%

Fiber 1g4%

Sugar 57g63%

Protein 15g30%

Nutrient A 445IU9%

Nutrient C 5.9mg7%

Calcium 254mg25%

Iron 5.2mg29%

Instructions

1. Clean the shrimp and put it in a safe spot.

2. In a little bowl, whisk the coconut milk and season with salt and pepper. Put in a safe spot. In a different little bowl, whisk together the coconut, panko, cayenne pepper, salt, and pepper.

3. One at once, plunge the shrimp in the coconut milk, the panko, and afterward place in the bin of the fryer. Rehash until all the shrimp are covered. Cook the shrimp in the air fryer for about

twenty minutes at 350 degrees or until the shrimp are cooked through.

4. Then, whisk together the preserves, nectar, mustard, and hot sauce.

5. Serve the shrimp with the sauce right away.

Air Fryer Baked Sweet Potato

Ingredients

• 3 sweet potatoes

• 1 tablespoon olive oil

• 1-2 teaspoons fit salt

Instructions

1. Wash your sweet potatoes and afterward make air gaps with a fork in the potatoes.

2. Sprinkle them with the olive oil and salt, at that point rub equitably on the potatoes.

3. Once the potatoes are covered, spot them into the container for the Air Fryer and spot it into the machine.

4. Cook the potatoes at 390 degrees for forty minutes or until fork delicate.

Air Fryer Jalapeno Poppers

1. Mix 1/2 of morsels and cream cheddar. When consolidated, include the parsley.

2. Stuff each pepper with this blend.

3. Gently press the highest points of the peppers into the staying 1/4 c of pieces to make the top covering.

4. Cook in an air fryer at 360 degrees F for 8 minutes.

Above all else, start with some crisp jalapenos. Know that not all jalapenos are made equivalent! I've eaten some that are mellow, some that have no zest by any means, and ones that will genuinely take your breath away!

Also, truly, that is the best part about jalapenos. With every single nibble, you have no clue really what sort of flavor you will get!

In the wake of choosing your peppers, remove the tops, and remember that you have to de-seed them! Significant advance! Also, another little tip?

Wear gloves while doing this progression. So often, I've cut open that jalapeno pepper, at that point overlooks and cleaned my eyes later. The agony! It truly will consume for quite a long time.

Ingredients

- 10 jalapeno peppers divided and deseeded

- 8 oz of cream cheddar I utilized a sans dairy cream cheddar

- 1/4 c crisp parsley

- 3/4 c sans gluten tortilla or bread morsels

Instructions

1. Mix 1/2 of scraps and cream cheddar. When joined, including the parsley.

2. Stuff each pepper with this blend.

3. Gently press the highest points of the peppers into the staying 1/4 c of morsels to make the top covering.

4. Cook in an air fryer at 370 degrees F for 6-8 minutes OR in a regular oven at 375 degrees F for 20 minutes.

Air Fryer Pork Taquitos

Ingredients

• 30 oz. of cooked destroyed pork tenderloin (not a fanatic of Pork? Utilize the destroyed chicken!)

• 2 1/2 cups fat-free destroyed mozzarella

• 10 little flour tortillas

• 1 lime, squeezed

• Cooking shower

• Salsa for plunging (discretionary)

• Sour Cream (discretionary)

• OMORC Air Fryer

Directions

• Slightly heat air fryer to 380 degrees.

• Sprinkle lime squeeze over pork and delicately blend around.

• Microwave 5 tortillas one after another with a clammy paper towel over it for 10 seconds, to mollify.

• Add 3 oz. of pork and then 1/3 cup of cheddar to a tortilla.

• Tightly and tenderly move up the tortillas.

• Line tortillas on a lubed foil-lined dish.

• Spray an even layer of cooking splash over tortillas.

• Air Fry for about 8 minutes until tortillas are a brilliant shading, flipping part of the way through.

Ingredients

• 3 cups cooked destroyed pork tenderloin or chicken

• 2 1/2 cups fat-free destroyed mozzarella

• 10 little flour tortillas

• 1 lime, squeezed

• Cooking splash

Instructions

1. Slightly heat air fryer to 380 degrees.

2. Sprinkle lime squeeze over pork and tenderly blend around.

3. Microwave 5 tortillas one after another with a soggy paper towel over it for 10 seconds, to mellow.

4. Add 3 oz. of pork and 1/4 cup of cheddar to a tortilla.

5. Tightly and tenderly move up the tortillas.

6. Line tortillas on a lubed foil-lined dish.

7. Spray an even layer of cooking splash over tortillas.

8. Air Fry for 7-10 minutes until tortillas are a brilliant shading, flipping part of the way through.

9. 2 taquitos per serving WW SP - 8.

10. But if you don't have an air fryer, they can likewise be heated in the oven for 7 - 10 minutes on 375 degrees.

Notes

1. Recommend 2 taquitos per serving

2. Add discretionary things like salsa or acrid cream to plunge!

3. Serve with guacamole and make a light supper that everybody will cherish.

4. Weight Watchers Smart Points determined to utilize the Weight Watchers formula developer.

Beetroot Chips

Ingredients

• 2 Medium Sized Beetroot

• 1/2 Tsp Oil

• Salt to taste

• Pepper Optional

Instructions

1. Wash the Beetroot, strip the skin, and put the skin in a safe spot. Utilizing a mandoline slicer, cut them flimsy. Also, if there is no slicer, cut them consistently slightly with your blade.

2. Use the skin to color your prop if you need to or dump it into your food squander.

3. Spread the beetroot cuts on the paper and spot another paper on it. Save it aside for 10 minutes. This procedure will empower

to assimilate any additional dampness on the beetroot diminishes.

4. Toss the cut beetroot in oil and sprinkle the required salt on the beetroot.

5. Slightly heat the Airfryer to 150 C for 4 minutes. Pull the crate from the air fryer and spot the chips in them. Slide it back in the air fryer and fry for 1about five minutes. Make a point to expel in the middle of after at regular intervals and give it a decent shake. When the chips are marginally fresh on the external edges and delicate in the center, permit them to chill off for quite a while.

6. Slide the bushel with the chips back again and warmth at 180 C for an additional 3 minutes. The chips will be truly fresh in general and immaculate to much immediately.

7. Season with Sea Salt and crisply ground pepper if you like or simply chew it all things considered. We love it in any case.

Fryer Shishito Peppers

This Keto cordial formula is a snappy, simple, flavorful low carb canapé for any social occasion or even only a peaceful night plunk down with your darling and a glass of wine!

Ingredients

- 1 6 oz sack Shishito peppers

- salt and pepper to taste

- 1/2 tbsp avocado oil

- 1/3 cup Asiago Cheese, ground fine

- Limes

Instructions

1. Rinse the peppers with water and then spot in a bowl, and hurl with avocado oil, salt, and pepper. Spot in the air fryer and cook at 350 for 10 minutes. Watch cautiously. You need them to turn out rankled looking yet not consumed.

2. Place shishito peppers on serving platter. Shower with a little lime squeezed and topped with ground asiago cheddar. Serve!

Notes

Around seven peppers for each serving. Fat 4g, Net Carb 1g, Protein 3g

Sustenance data determined to utilize myfitnesspal is given as an obligingness, yet will differ contingent upon the particular brands of ingredients you use.

Sustenance Information:

Yield: 4

Sum Per Serving: Calories: 63

Sustenance data is given as a friendship; however, it will change contingent upon the particular brands of ingredients you use if it's not too much trouble counsel with your primary care physician in regards to explicit wellbeing needs.

Air Fryer Bacon Wrapped Scallops

Messing with them in my kitchen, I discovered somewhat cooking the bacon before wrapping the scallops gives you the best outcomes for consummately cooked scallops and fresh bacon.

Cooking Tips

• For splendidly cooked scallops, make certain to pat the scallops dry. Spot them between paper towels to get any dampness out.

• One-half cut of bacon fit flawlessly around each scallop, you'll need a toothpick to make sure about it.

• Always turn your food midway when air browning. The warming component is at the top, so turning it will prepare food equally on the two sides.

Looking all starry eyed at air broiling:

• Food turns out such a great amount of crispier than it does in my oven.

• It takes just three minutes to Slightly heat up, and it doesn't warm up the kitchen.

• It's more secure and more beneficial than profound broiling, and it doesn't smoke up the entire house.

• The air fryer has now supplanted my oven on most weekdays and evenings, in the case of making hard bubbled eggs, preparing a side dish, warming up remains, or making dinner.

Ingredients

• 16 enormous ocean scallops, cleaned and pat dry with paper towels

• Eight cuts focus cut bacon

• 16 toothpicks

• Olive oil shower

• Freshly ground dark pepper, to taste.

Instructions

1. Slightly heat air fryer to 400F 3 minutes.

2. Place the bacon inside the air fryer to partially cook about 3 minutes, turning midway. Evacuate and set on a paper towel to cool.

3. Remove the side muscles of the scallops. Dry with paper towels to expel any dampness.

4. Wrap each scallop in the cut of bacon and secure it with a toothpick.

5. Spritz olive oil over scallops and season delicately with dark pepper.

6. Arrange scallops in a solitary layer in the air fryer, cook, in bunches 8 minutes turning most of the way until scallop is delicate and misty and bacon is cooked through and serve when hot.

Air Fryer Mozzarella Sticks

Ingredients

• 1 (12-ounce) bundle mozzarella cheddar sticks, each stick opened up and cut down the middle to make 12 sticks

• 1/4 cup mayonnaise

• 1 enormous egg

- 1/4 cup universally handy flour

- 1/4 cup fine, dry breadcrumbs

- 1/2 teaspoon onion powder

- 1/2 teaspoon garlic powder

- 1 cup marinara sauce, for serving

Instructions

1. Before singing, place the divided cheddar sticks on a rimmed preparing sheet fixed with material paper. Freeze for 30 minutes. In the meantime, collect the breading and get out the air fryer.

2. Spot the flour, breadcrumbs, onion, and garlic powder in an enormous bowl and speed to join.

3. Working in clusters of 6, roll the solidified cheddar sticks in the mayo-egg blend to cover, at that point in the flour blend. Return the covered cheddar adheres to the material lined preparing sheet. Rehash with the rest of the cheddar sticks. Return the heating sheet to the cooler for 10 minutes.

4. Heat the air fryer to about 360°F. Fry the mozzarella sticks for about five minutes - it is significant not to stuff the air fryer. Rehash with the rest of the sticks and serve warm with the marinara for plunging.

Air Fryer Tater Tots

Why These Air Fryer Tater Tots Are So Good!

• This is a more beneficial method for cooking a most loved game day tidbit and side dish.

• It just takes 1about five minutes to cook the potato tots from solidified.

• They are truly tasty! They taste pan-fried however are such a lot more beneficial!

• You just need three ingredients for fantastically firm tots!

Instructions to Make Air Fryer Tater Tots

1. Slightly heat air fryer to 400°f if your AF needs that.

2. Coat the tots with a bit of cooking splash, similar to avocado oil. Sprinkle with salt and hurl to cover. These means produce the best air fryer potato tots.

3. Cook for 1about five minutes on 400°f – flip them in the container like clockwork or so until fresh and brilliant and medium dark-colored in a couple of spots

4. Add additional time if you need them crispier

Potato Tot Recipe, Fried Tater Tots, Healthier Tater Tots Recipe

Ingredients

• 16 ounces solidified potato tots

• Avocado oil (or another cooking splash)

• Salt

Instructions

1. Slightly heat your air fryer to 400°f.

2. Coat the solidified tots with a touch of the cooking shower, similar to avocado oil. Sprinkle with salt and hurl to cover.

3. Cook for 1about five minutes on 400°f – flip them in the crate like clockwork or so until fresh and brilliant and medium dark-colored in a couple of spots.

4. Add additional time if you need them crispier.

Notes

I suggest utilizing natural solidified potato tots for the most beneficial rendition.

This is the air fryer I use.

Keto Coconut Shrimp

I prodded this keto coconut shrimp formula on Instagram a week ago, and you all went crazy! I had no real option except to share the low carb formula with you, and you have the choice of cooking the coconut shrimp in the air fryer or sautéed. The way to making this keto is supplanting panko bread morsels with squashed pork skins! They are low carb, salty, and crunchy.

Making Low Carb Coconut Shrimp?

The initial step to making coconut shrimp is setting up a dig station. This will comprise of prepared coconut flour, beaten eggs, and 1/2 cup every one of squashed pork skins and unsweetened coconut drops. Season the shrimp with a touch of salt and afterward dig in the coconut flour, the eggs, and the panko blend.

I will likewise incorporate the conventional coconut shrimp formula down underneath, including the macros for every procedure. This technique utilizes generally useful flour and panko bread morsels.

Permit the battered shrimp to sit on a wire rack for 10 minutes so the covering can solidify and truly adhere to the shrimp. Meanwhile, you can make the plunging sauce.

Make Coconut Shrimp Sauce

Making a low carb sauce that pairs mind the fried coconut shrimp, join mayonnaise, ground garlic, lime get-up-and-go and squeeze, and sriracha in a little bowl. You can modify the measure of sriracha dependent on how hot you like it.

Commonly coconut shrimp is paired with a sweet stew sauce, yet that is stacked with sugar and not keto agreeable.

Instructions to Fry Coconut Shrimp In The Air Fryer

There are two strategies to broil the coconut shrimp. The first alternative is to utilize the air fryer. Splash container with non-stick, and cook at 390 degrees F for 8 minutes, flipping midway. The shrimp will be brilliant dark-colored and fresh when prepared.

To sauté the low carb coconut shrimp, pre-heat two creeps of oil in a fried dish until it arrives at 350 degrees F. Fry the shrimp for 2-3 minutes on each side or until brilliant dark-colored. Expel from the skillet and spot on a wire rack set in a sheet plate. When the shrimp are prepared, sprinkle a little spot of salt over the top while they are hot.

Would I be able to Use Frozen Shrimp To Make Coconut Shrimp?

You can utilize solidified shrimp. Simply try to defrost them under virus running water and pat them dry before covering with the hitter. Don't utilize pre-cooked shrimp as they will get over-cooked and extreme once they are fried.

Ingredients

For the shrimp:

- 1 pound shrimp stripped and cleaned

- ¾ cup universally handy flour

- 1 teaspoon every onion and garlic powder

- 2 eggs gently beaten

- ½ cup each panko breadcrumbs and unsweetened destroyed coconut pieces

- Kosher salt and crisp pepper

- Avocado or grapeseed oil

- ½ cup full-fat mayonnaise

- Zest and juice of a large portion of a lime

- One clove garlic finely ground

- 2-3 tablespoons sriracha or hot sauce

For the keto coconut shrimp:

• ¾ cup coconut flour

• 1 teaspoon every onion and garlic powder

• 2 eggs softly beaten

• ½ cup every pork skin morsels and unsweetened destroyed coconut chips

• Kosher salt and crisp pepper

Avocado or grapeseed oil

Instructions

1. For the keto coconut shrimp, set up the dig station by including the coconut flour, onion and garlic powder, ½ teaspoon salt, and a couple of breaks of pepper to a shallow dish, blend well. Add the eggs to a little dish/bowl and softly whisk. Add the pork skins to a zip-top pack and utilize a folding pin to slam them into breadcrumbs the size of panko. Add them to a dish alongside the coconut pieces, ¼ teaspoon salt, not many breaks of pepper, and blend well.

2. Season the shrimp with a little touch of salt on both sides at that point, dig in the coconut flour shake off any abundance, dig in the eggs, shake off any overabundance, dig in the pork skin and coconut drops and ensure the shrimp is all around secured. Repeat with the rest of the shrimp.

3. For the standard adaptation of the coconut shrimp, follow the equivalent precise advances, yet all of you reason flour rather than coconut and panko breadcrumbs rather than pork skins.

4. Pour two creeps of oil into a grill and carry the temperature to 340-350 F. While the oil is coming to temperature, it's alright that the shrimp sit at room temperature so the covering can firm up. Fry the shrimp in groups, for 2-3 minutes on each side, or until brilliant dark-colored. Expel shrimp and spot on a perfect wire rack and fry the following clump.

5. Make the sriracha plunging sauce by joining all the ingredients in a little bowl and whisking admirably. Check for flavoring, and you may require more sriracha if you like it zesty.

6. If utilizing an air fryer to make the coconut shrimp, shower the container with non-stick and fry for 8 minutes at 390 F, flipping the shrimp midway.

Nourishment

Macros per keto coconut shrimp:

75 calories

0.9 net carbs

2 grams of absolute carbs

4 grams of fat

3.2 grams of protein

1.6 grams of fiber

Macros per customary coconut shrimp:

70 calories

5 grams of carbs

3 grams of fat

3 grams of protein

0.5 grams of fiber

Keto Coconut Shrimp

Sum Per Serving

Calories 75 Calories from Fat 36

% Daily Value*

Fat 4g6%

Sugars 2g1%

Fiber 1.6g7%

Protein 3.2g6%

Percent Daily Values depend on a 2000 calorie diet.

Air Fryer Buffalo Cauliflower Bites

Cauliflower remains a flavorful veggie-lover option in contrast to chicken wings right now, zesty Air Fryer Buffalo Cauliflower

Bites. Arranged with an almond flour breading and a rich hot sauce, these cauliflower chomps are low carb, Keto-accommodating, thus heavenly!!

Making Buffalo Cauliflower Bites in the Air Fryer

1. Cut up the cauliflower into florets and put those in an enormous blending bowl.

2. Next, soften some margarine and blend in a decent portion of hot sauce into it.

3. Pour the hot sauce blend over the cauliflower florets and blend them around. I utilize my hands for this part. However, I make a point to wash my hands multiple times in the wake of blending since it would freakin' HURT if I ignited my eyes without washing the hot sauce first. Been there, done that... although everything recollects it.

4. Then, you'll need to whisk together a touch of almond flour with flavoring salt, garlic powder, and dried parsley.

5. Sprinkle that over the cauliflower florets – utilize a bunch of almond flour blend at once and just delicately mix them around with the goal that all florets are covered.

6. Air Fry HALF of the cauliflower chomps at 350°F (no compelling reason to Slightly heat up) for around 1about five minutes. Stop and shake two or multiple times during the cooking procedure.

7. Evacuate the cauliflower from the air fryer and keep secure while you cook the subsequent bunch.

8. Serve promptly with a side of celery sticks and bleu cheddar dressing—also, increasingly hot sauce.

Tips For Air Fryer Buffalo Cauliflower Bites

1. DO NOT swarm the air fryer dish. If you swarm it, the cauliflower nibbles will turn out saturated. This is the reason you need to cook the cauliflower in two clumps. You have to have enough air stream to go all around each piece.

2. If you're not happy with the crunch, put cauliflower nibbles under the grill for 2 minutes, at that point serve.

Step by step instructions to Make In The Oven

• Place arranged cauliflower florets on a foil-lined container and heat for 1about five minutes at 450°F. Delicately mix cauliflower part of the way through cooking.

Step by step instructions to Make Ahead

• Buffalo Cauliflower Bites are likewise extraordinary to make ahead. Set up every component in advance – cut up the cauliflower, cause the sauce, to set up the breading – and keep them in isolated compartments until prepared to utilize. You WILL need to warm up the hot sauce and give it a decent mix before utilizing it.

Instructions to Store Leftovers

• While Cauliflower Bites taste best when served quickly, you can, in any case, refrigerate the scraps in an airtight holder for as long as two days.

Ingredient

• 1 head cauliflower (around 4 to 5 cups)

• 2 tablespoons margarine, liquefied

• 1 tablespoon olive oil

• 1/2 cup Frank's Red Hot Sauce

- 1/2 cup almond flour

- 3 tablespoons dried parsley

- 1/2 tablespoon garlic powder

- 1 teaspoon Lawry's Seasoning Salt

Instructions

1. Place cauliflower florets in an enormous blending bowl and put it in a safe spot.

2. Melt margarine; mix in olive oil and hot sauce until altogether consolidated.

3. Pour the hot sauce blend over the cauliflower; blend around until all cauliflower florets are covered.

4. In a different bowl, whisk together almond flour, dried parsley, garlic powder, and flavoring salt.

5. Sprinkle about a bunch during a period of almond flour blend over the cauliflower; tenderly blend until everything is covered.

6. Transfer portion of the readied cauliflower to the air fryer.

7. Air fry at 350°F for 1about five minutes, shaking two or multiple times during the cooking procedure. Cauliflower is done when the florets are somewhat caramelized, however not soft.

8. Remove cauliflower from the Air Fryer; put in a safe spot and keep secure.

9. Repeat a similar procedure with the rest of the cauliflower florets.

10. Serve with celery sticks and your preferred bleu cheddar dressing.

Air Fryer Buffalo Cauliflower Bites

1. DO NOT swarm the air fryer dish. If you swarm it, the cauliflower nibbles will turn out spongy. This is the reason you need to cook the cauliflower in two clusters. You have to have enough air stream to go all around each piece.

2. For more crunch, put cauliflower chomps under the oven for 2 minutes, at that point serve.

The most effective method to MAKE IN THE OVEN

• Place arranged cauliflower florets on a foil-lined dish and prepare for 1about five minutes at 450°F. Tenderly mix the cauliflower part of the way through cooking.

Nourishment Facts; Air Fryer Buffalo Cauliflower Bites

Sum Per Serving

Calories 204 Calories from Fat 153

% Daily Value*

Fat 17g26%

Soaked Fat 5g25%

Cholesterol 15mg5%

Sodium 1602mg67%

Potassium 482mg14%

Starches 12g4%

Fiber 5g20%

Sugar 3g3%

Protein 6g12%

Nutrient A 204IU4%

Nutrient C 71mg86%

Calcium 78mg8%

Iron 2mg11%

Percent Daily Values depend on a 2000 calorie diet.

CHAPTER FIVE

SNACKS RECIPES

Peach Hand Pies in an Air Fryer

Normally, new peaches will make the best filling. However, you can utilize defrosted solidified peaches if the crisp kind isn't in season. Try not to hurl out the remaining peach juice—stew it down in a little pan until thickened for a fabulous frozen yogurt topper.

Ingredients

• 2 (5-oz.) crisp peaches, stripped and cleaved

• 1 tablespoon crisp lemon juice (from 1 lemon)

• 3 tablespoons granulated sugar

• 1 teaspoon vanilla concentrate

• 1/4 teaspoon table salt

• 1 teaspoon cornstarch

• 1 (14.1-oz.) pkg. refrigerated piecrusts

Nourishing Information

Calories 314 Fat 16g Sat fat 7g UnSat fat 7g Protein 3g Carbohydrate 43g Fiber 1g Sugars 10g Added sugars 6g Sodium 347mg Calcium 0% DV Potassium 2% DV

Direction

1. Stir together peaches, lemon juice, sugar, vanilla, and salt an in medium bowl. Let stand 1about five minutes, blending once in a

while. Channel peaches, holding 1 tablespoon fluid. Whisk cornstarch into the saved fluid; mix into depleted peaches.

2. Cut piecrusts into 8 (4-inch) circles. The spot around 1 tablespoon filling in the focus of each circle. Brush edges of batter with water; overlap mixture over filling to frame half-moons. Crease edges with a fork to seal; cut three little cuts in top of pies— coat pies well with cooking splash.

Spot 3 pies in a single layer in air fryer bushel, and cook at 350°F until brilliant dark colored, 12 to 14 minutes. Rehash with residual pies.

Empanadas in an Air Fryer

Conventional meat-filled empanadas can be a one-two punch of fat and calories because of ground hamburger and an outing to the profound fryer; This air fryer wind is much more beneficial gratitude to the expansion of mushrooms, which help the filling while at the same time keeping it decent and wet. We love the rich kind of Castelvetrano olives. However, you can utilize any green olives you have close by. These handheld tidbits are extraordinary for closely following, or serve them over greens for a generous dinner.

Ingredients

- 1 tablespoon olive oil

- 3 ounces (85/15) lean ground meat

- 1/4 cup finely hacked white onion

- 3 ounces finely hacked cremini mushrooms

- 2 teaspoons finely hacked garlic

- 6 pitted green olives, hacked

- 1/4 teaspoon paprika

- 1/4 teaspoon ground cumin

- 1/8 teaspoon ground cinnamon

- 1/2 cup hacked tomatoes

- 8 square gyoza wrappers

- 1 huge egg, daintily beaten

Dietary Information

Calories 343 Fat 19g Sat fat 5g UnSat Fat 12g Protein 17g Carbohydrate 25g Fiber 2g Sugars 3g Added sugars 0g Sodium 605mg Calcium 6% DV Potassium 12% DV

Direction

1. Heat the oil and include meat and onion; cook, mixing to disintegrate, until beginning to dark-colored, 3 minutes. Include mushrooms; cook, blending at times until mushrooms are beginning to dark-colored, 6 minutes. Include garlic, olives, paprika, cumin, and cinnamon; cook until mushrooms are extremely delicate and have discharged a large portion of their fluid, 3 minutes. Mix in tomatoes, and cook one moment, mixing once in a while. Move to fill to a bowl, and let cool about five minutes.

2. Arrange four gyoza wrappers on work surface. The spot around 1/2 tablespoons filling in the focus of every wrapper. Brush edges of wrappers with egg; overlap wrappers over, squeezing edges to seal. Rehash process with residual wrappers and filling.

3. Place four empanadas in a single layer in air fryer crate, and cook at 400°F until pleasantly sautéed 7 minutes. Rehash with remaining empanadas.

Air Fryer Fried Ravioli Recipe

Ingredients in toasted ravioli:

• Refrigerated cheddar ravioli

• Eggs

• Breadcrumbs

• Panko

• Parmesan

• Onion powder

• Garlic powder

• Salt

• Dried basil

• Italian flavoring

How would you make air fryer fried ravioli?

1. In a medium – huge bowl, beat together two eggs.

2. In another medium – huge bowl, whisk together breadcrumbs, panko, parmesan, onion powder, garlic powder, salt, dried basil, and Italian flavoring.

3. Whisk the egg in a bowl and mix until every ravioli is completely covered.

4. Place in the breadcrumb blend and coat until all the kinds of ravioli are completely secured.

5. Slightly heat air fryer to 400 degrees F and splash the bushel with cooking shower.

6. Place nine covered kinds of ravioli in a solitary layer (pretty much relying upon the size of your air fryer), and air fry for 3 minutes, or until toasty and warm.

7. Don't over air fry or the cheddar will break out.

8. Serve and appreciate it!

Would I be able to make fried ravioli in the oven?

1. Line a rimmed heating sheet with a silicone preparing mat.

2. Place covered ravioli in a solitary layer on the readied heating sheet. Discretionary: shower gently with cooking splash.

3. Bake for 10-1about five minutes, delicately flipping partially through, or until the ravioli is warm and fresh.

4. Serve and appreciate it!

Ingredients

• 1 (20 oz) bundle refrigerated cheddar ravioli I utilized Buitoni 4 Cheese Ravioli and would suggest this for best outcomes (see interface)

• 2 huge eggs

• 1/2 cup breadcrumbs

• 1/2 cup panko

- 1/4 cup ground parmesan

- 1 teaspoon onion powder

- 1 teaspoon garlic powder

- 1 teaspoon dried basil

- 1/2 teaspoon Italian flavoring

- 1/2 teaspoon salt pretty much to taste

- Marinara sauce for plunging

- Alfredo sauce for plunging

Instructions

1. Whisk the eggs together in a medium - tremendous bowl. Put in a protected spot.

2. Place breadcrumbs, panko, dried basil, parmesan, onion powder, garlic powder, and salt in another medium - gigantic bowl. Surge until particularly merged. Put in a sheltered spot.

3. Place ravioli in the whisked egg bowl and blend until each ravioli is secured.

4. Place in the breadcrumb mix and coat until all the ravioli are made sure about.

5. Set aside on an immaculate work surface.

For the air fryer:

1. Slightly warm up air fryer to 400 degrees F and give carton cooking sprinkle.

2. Working with nine on the double, lay the canvassed ravioli in a singular layer. Optional: sprinkle ravioli gently with cooking shower.

3. Close the air fryer and the air fryer for 3 minutes, or until the ravioli is warm and new.

4. Repeat with lingering ravioli.

5. Serve with plunging sauce of choice.

For the oven:

1. Slightly warmth up oven to 400 degrees F and line a rimmed warming sheet with a silicone tangle.

2. Lay the shrouded ravioli in a single layer onto the prepared warming sheet. Optional: shower ravioli gently with a cooking sprinkle.

3. Bake in Slightly heat the oven for 10-1about five minutes, or until the ravioli is warm and new.

4. Serve with plunging sauce of decision.

Notes

Don't overheat/air fry, or the cheddar will vanish. Diminish or include cooking time based on the size of your ravioli.

Air Fryer Churros With Chocolate Sauce

Kefir is a dairy item like yogurt that is a lot more slender (it's drinkable, similar to a smoothie) and pressed with gut-sound probiotics. The somewhat tart flavor makes the chocolate sauce pleasant and smooth. Make certain to cool the mixture before channeling to assist it withholding its shape in the air fryer craze.

You'll appreciate the churros promptly as they're the best crisp. However, you can spare any additional chocolate sauce—have a go at sprinkling it over solidified yogurt.

Ingredients

- 1/2 cup water

- 1/4 teaspoon legitimate salt

- 1/4 cup, in addition to 2 Tbsp. unsalted spread, separated

- 1/2 cup (around 2 1/8 oz.) generally useful flour

- 2 huge eggs

- 1/3 cup granulated sugar

- 2 teaspoons ground cinnamon

- 4 ounces ambivalent preparing chocolate, finely slashed

- 3 tablespoons substantial cream

- 2 tablespoons vanilla kefir

Direction

1. Take salt, water, and 1/3 cup of the margarine to a bubble in a little pan over medium-high. Decrease warmth to medium-low; include flour, and mix enthusiastically with a wooden spoon until the mixture is smooth around 30 seconds. Keep cooking, mixing continually until the mixture starts to pull away from sides of the dish and a film frames on the base of the container, 2 to 3 minutes. Move batter to a medium bowl. Mix continually until marginally cooled, around one moment. Include eggs, 1 at once, mixing continually until totally smooth after every expansion. Move blend to a funneling pack fitted with a medium star tip. Chill 30 minutes.

2. Pipe 6 pieces in a single layer in the air fryer container. Cook at 380°F until brilliant, around 10 minutes. Rehash with the residual mixture.

3. Stir the sugar with the cinnamon in a bowl. Brush cooked churros with staying 2 tablespoons softened margarine, and move in sugar blend to cover.

4. Place chocolate and cream in a little microwavable bowl. Microwave on HIGH until dissolved and smooth, around 30

seconds, mixing the following 15 seconds. Mix in kefir. Serve churros with chocolate sauce.

Air Fryer Doughnuts Have Just 4g of Fat.

Ingredients

• 1/4 cup warm water, warmed (100F to 110F)

• 1 teaspoon dynamic dry yeast

• 1/4 cup, in addition to 1/2 tsp. granulated sugar, separated

• 2 cups (around 8 1/2 oz.) generally useful flour

• 1/4 teaspoon legitimate salt

• 1/4 cup entire milk, at room temperature

• 2 tablespoons unsalted spread, dissolved

• 1 huge egg, beaten

• 1 cup (around 4 oz.) powdered sugar

• 4 teaspoons faucet water

Healthful Information

Calories 238 Fat 4g Sat fat 2g UnSat fat 1g Protein 5g Carbohydrate 46g Fiber 1g Sugars 22g Added Sugars 21g Sodium 74mg Calcium 2% DV Potassium 1% DV

Direction

1. Stir together water, yeast, and 1/2 teaspoon of the granulated sugar in a little bowl; let remain until frothy, around about five minutes. Join flour, salt, and staying 1/4 cup granulated sugar in a medium bowl. Include yeast blend, milk, spread, and egg; mix with a wooden spoon until a delicate mixture meets up. Turn batter out onto a gently floured surface and work until smooth, 1 to 2 minutes. Move batter to a gently lubed bowl. Spread and let ascend in a warm spot until multiplied in volume, around 60 minutes.

2. Turn batter out onto a delicately floured surface. Tenderly move to 1/4-inch thickness. Cut out 8 doughnuts utilizing a 3-inch round shaper and a 1-inch round shaper to expel focus. Spot doughnuts and doughnuts gaps on a gently floured surface.

Spread freely with cling wrap and let remain until multiplied in volume, around 30 minutes.

3. Place 2 doughnuts and 2 doughnuts openings in a single layer in air fryer crate, and cook at 350°F until brilliant dark colored, 4 to about five minutes. Rehash with outstanding doughnuts and gaps.

4. Whisk together powdered sugar and faucet water in a medium bowl until smooth. Plunge doughnuts and donut gaps in the coat; place on a wire rack set over a rimmed heating sheet to permit abundance coating to dribble off. Let remain until coat solidifies, around 10 minutes.

Air-Fried Curry Chickpeas Make the Perfect Crispy Snack

Ingredients

• 1 (15-oz.) can no-salt-included chickpeas (garbanzo beans), depleted and flushed (around 1/2 cups)

• 2 tablespoons red wine vinegar

- 2 tablespoons olive oil

- 2 teaspoons curry powder

- 1/2 teaspoon ground turmeric

- 1/4 teaspoon ground coriander

- 1/4 teaspoon ground cumin

- 1/4 teaspoon in addition to 1/8 tsp. ground cinnamon

- 1/4 teaspoon fit salt

- 1/2 teaspoon Aleppo pepper

- Thinly cut new cilantro.

Healthful Information

Calories 173 Fat 8g Sat fat 1g UnSat fat 6g Protein 7g Carbohydrate 18g Fiber 5g Sugars 1g Added sugars 0g Sodium 146mg Calcium 6% DV Potassium 4% DV

Direction

1. Gently crush chickpeas with your hands in a medium bowl (don't smash); dispose of chickpea skins.

2. Add vinegar and oil to chickpeas, and hurl to cover. Include curry powder, turmeric, coriander, cumin, and cinnamon; mix delicately to consolidate.

3. Place chickpeas in a single layer in air fryer container, and cook at 400°F until firm, around 1about five minutes, shaking chickpeas partially through cooking.

4. Transfer chickpeas to a bowl. Sprinkle with salt, Aleppo pepper, and cilantro; hurl to cover.

CHAPTER SIX

DESSERTS

Air Fryer Apple Pies

Ingredients

• 4 tablespoons margarine

• 6 tablespoons darker sugar

• 1 teaspoon ground cinnamon

• 2 medium Granny Smith apples, diced

• 1 teaspoon cornstarch

• 2 teaspoons cold water

• 1/2 (14 ounces) bundle cake for a 9-inch twofold outside layer pie

• Cooking splash

• 1/2 tablespoon grapeseed oil

• 1/4 cup powdered sugar

• 1 teaspoon milk, or more varying

Directions

1. Combine apples, spread, darker sugar, and cinnamon in a non-stick skillet. Cook over medium warmth until apples have mollified, around about five minutes.

2. Dissolve corn-starch in chilly water. Mix into apple blend and cook until sauce thickens, around 1 moment. Expel crusty fruit-

filled treat filling from the warmth and put aside to cool while you set up the hull.

3. Unroll pie outside on a gently floured surface and turn out somewhat to smooth the outside of the batter. Cut the mixture into square shapes sufficiently little, so 2 can fit in your air fryer at once. Rehash with residual outside layer until you have 8 equivalent square shapes, removing a portion of the pieces of the mixture if necessary.

4. Wet the external edges of 4 square shapes with water and spot some apple filling in the middle around 1/2-inch from the edges. Reveal the staying 4 square shapes with the goal that they are somewhat bigger than the filled ones. Spot these square shapes on the filling; crease the edges with a fork to seal. Cut 4 little cuts in the highest points of the pies.

5. Spray the container of an air fryer with cooking splash. Brush the highest points of 2 pies with grape seed oil and move pies to the air fryer container utilizing a spatula.

6. Insert container and set the temperature to 385 degrees F (195 degrees C). Prepare until brilliant darker, around 8 minutes. Expel pies from the bin and rehash with the staying 2 pies.

7. Mix the powdered sugar and the milk in a little bowl. Brush coat on warm pies and permit to dry. Serve pies warm or at room temperature.

Sustenance Facts

Per Serving: 498 calories; 28.6 g fat; 59.8 g sugars; 3.3 g protein; 31 mg cholesterol; 328 mg sodium.

Air Fryer Oreos

Ingredients

• 1/2 cup total hotcake blend

• 1/3 cup water

• Cooking shower

• 9 chocolate sandwich treats, (for example, Oreo®)

• 1 tablespoon confectioners' sugar, or to taste

Directions

1. Mix flapjack blend and water until all around consolidated.

2. Line an air fryer crate with material paper. Splash material paper with nonstick cooking shower. Dunk every treat into the hotcake blend and spot in the bushel. Ensure they are not contacting; cook in clusters if important.

3. Slightly heat the air fryer to 400 degrees F. Include container and cook for 4 to about five minutes; flip and cook until brilliant dark colored, 2 to 3 minutes more. Sprinkle with confectioners' sugar.

Air Fryer Churros

Ingredients

- 1/4 cup spread

- 1/2 cup milk

- 1 squeeze salt

- 1/2 cup universally handy flour

- 2 eggs

- 1/4 cup white sugar

- 1/2 teaspoon ground cinnamon

Directions

1. Melt margarine in a pan over medium-high warmth. Pour in milk and include salt. Lower warmth to medium and heat to the point of boiling, consistently mixing with a wooden spoon. Rapidly include flour at the same time. Continue blending until the mixture meets up.

2. Remove from warmth and let cool for 5 to 7 minutes. Blend in eggs with the wooden spoon until choux cake meets up. Spoon batter into a cake sack fitted with a huge star tip—Channel mixture into strips straight into the air fryer container.

3. Air fry churros at 340 degrees F (175 degrees C) for about five minutes.

4. Meanwhile, join sugar and cinnamon in a little bowl and pour it onto a shallow plate.

5. Remove fried churros from the air fryer and move in the cinnamon-sugar blend.

Sustenance Facts

Per Serving: 172 calories; 9.8 g fat; 17.5 g sugars; 3.9 g protein; 84 mg cholesterol; 112 mg sodium.

Air Fryer Apple Fritters

Ingredients

• cooking shower

• 1 cup universally handy flour

• 1/4 cup white sugar

• 1/4 cup milk

• 1 egg

• 1/2 teaspoons heating powder

- 1 squeeze salt

- 2 tablespoons white sugar

- 1/2 teaspoon ground cinnamon

- 1 apple - stripped, cored, and slashed

- Glaze:

- 1/2 cup confectioners' sugar

- 1 tablespoon milk

- 1/2 teaspoon caramel concentrate, (for example, Watkins™)

- 1/4 teaspoon ground cinnamon

Directions

1. Slightly heat an air fryer to about 340 degrees F . Spot a material paper round into the base of the air fryer—shower with nonstick cooking splash.

2. Mix flour, milk, egg, warming powder, 1/3 cup sugar, and salt together in a little bowl. Blend until combined.

3. Mix about three tablespoons of sugar with the cinnamon in another bowl and sprinkle over apples until secured. Mix apples into the flour mix until joined.

4. Drop abuses using a treat scoop onto the base of the air fryer canister.

5. Air-fry in the Slightly heat used fryer for around five minutes. Flip abuses and cook until splendid, around five minutes more.

6. Meanwhile, blend confectioners' sugar, milk, caramel concentrate, and cinnamon in a bowl. Move misuses to a cooling rack and sprinkle with a coat.

Nourishment

297 calories; 64.9 g starches; 5.5 g protein; 2.1 g fat; 48 mg cholesterol; 248 mg sodium.

Air Fryer Roasted Bananas

Ingredients

• 1 banana, cut into 1/8-inch thick diagonals

• Avocado oil cooking splash

Directions

1. Line air fryer bushel with material paper.

2. Slightly heat an air fryer to 375 degrees F (190 degrees C).

3. Place banana cuts into the bushel, ensuring that they are not contacting; cook in groups if fundamental. Fog banana cuts with avocado oil.

4. Cook them in the air fryer for about five minutes. Expel crate and flip banana cuts cautiously (they will be delicate). Cook until banana cuts are searing and caramelized, an extra 2 to 3 minutes. Cautiously expel from the bin.

Nourishment

107 calories; 27 g starches; 1.3 g protein; 0.7 g fat; 0 mg cholesterol; 1 mg sodium.

Air Fryer Beignets

Ingredients

- cooking splash

- 1/2 cup generally useful flour

- 1/4 cup white sugar

- 1/8 cup water

- 1 huge egg, isolated

- 1/2 teaspoons dissolved margarine

- 1/2 teaspoon preparing powder

- 1/2 teaspoon vanilla concentrate

- 1 squeeze salt

2 tablespoons confectioners' sugar, or to taste

Directions

1. Slightly heat air fryer to 370 degrees F. Splash the silicone egg-nibble form with nonstick cooking shower.

2. Whisk flour, sugar, heating powder, vanilla concentrate, water, egg yolk, spread, and salt together in a huge bowl. Mix to consolidate.

3. Beat egg white in a little bowl utilizing an electric hand blender on medium speed until delicate pinnacles structure. Crease into the player. Add hitter to the readied form utilizing a little pivoted dessert scoop.

4. Place filled silicone shape into the crate of the air fryer.

5. Fry in the Slightly heat used air fryer for 10 minutes. Expel shape from the crate cautiously; pop beignets out and flip over onto a material paper round.

6. Place material round with beignets once more into the air fryer container—Cook for an extra 4 minutes. Expel beignets from the air fryer container and residue with confectioners' sugar.

Air-Fried Banana Cake

Ingredients

• Cooking shower

• 1/3 cup darker sugar

• 3 1/2 tablespoons margarine, at room temperature

• 1 banana, pounded

• 1 egg

• 2 tablespoons nectar

• 1 cup self-rising flour

• 1/2 teaspoon ground cinnamon

• 1 squeeze salt

Directions

1. Slightly heat an air fryer to 320 degrees F (160 degrees C). Shower a little fluted tube container with a cooking splash.

2. Beat sugar and margarine together in a bowl utilizing an electric blender until rich. Consolidate banana, egg, and nectar in a different bowl. Whisk banana blend into spread blend until smooth.

3. Sift flour, cinnamon, and salt into the joined banana-margarine blend. Blend hitter until smooth. Move to the readied dish; level the surface utilizing the rear of a spoon.

4. Place the cake skillet in the air fryer bin. Slide the bushel into the air fryer and set the clock for 30 minutes. Prepare until a toothpick embedded into the cake tells the truth.

Note:

If you don't have an air fryer, this formula functions admirably in a toaster oven or ordinary oven. You can add about five minutes more to the cooking time.

Sustenance Facts

Per Serving: 347 calories; 11.8 g fat; 56.9 g sugars; 5.2 g protein; 73 mg cholesterol; 531 mg sodium.

Air-Fried Butter Cake

Ingredients

• Cooking shower

• 7 tablespoons margarine, at room temperature

• 1/4 cup white sugar

• 2 tablespoons white sugar

• 1 egg

• 1 2/3 cups universally handy flour

• 1 squeeze salt, or to taste

• 6 tablespoons milk

Directions

1. Slightly heat an air fryer to about 340 degrees F (180 degrees C). Shower a little fluted tube skillet with cooking splash.

2. Beat margarine and 1/4 cup in addition to 2 tablespoons spread together in a bowl utilizing an electric blender until light and rich. Include egg and blend until smooth and soft. Mix in flour and salt. Include milk and blend players altogether. Move player to the readied container; utilize the rear of a spoon to level the surface.

3. Place the container in the air fryer bushel. Set the clock for 1about five minutes. Heat until a toothpick embedded into the cake tells the truth.

4. Turn cake out of the container and permit to cool, around about five minutes.

Ingredients

• 1/3 cup spread

• 3 cups pitted fruits

• Ten tablespoons white sugar, partitioned

• 2 teaspoons lemon juice

• 1 cup without gluten universally handy heating flour

• 1 teaspoon vanilla powder

• 1 teaspoon ground nutmeg

• 1 teaspoon ground cinnamon

Directions

1. Cube spread and spot in cooler until firm, around 1about five minutes.

2. Slightly heat air fryer to 325 degrees F.

3. Combine pitted fruits, two tablespoons sugar, and lemon squeeze in a bowl; blend well. Empty cherry blend into a heating dish.

4. Mix the flour and 5 tablespoons of sugar in a bowl. Cut in margarine utilizing fingers until particles are pea-size. Convey over fruits and press down softly.

5. Stir 2 tablespoons sugar, vanilla powder, nutmeg, and cinnamon together in a bowl—residue sugar beating over the fruits and flour.

6. Bake in the Slightly heat used air fryer. Check at 2about five minutes; if not yet carmelized, keep cooking and checking at 5-minute interims until somewhat sautéed. Close cabinet and mood killer air fryer. Leave disintegrate inside for 10 minutes. Expel and permit to cool somewhat, around about five minutes.

Chocolate Cake in an Air Fryer

Ingredients

• Cooking splash

• 1/4 cup white sugar

• 3 1/2 tablespoons spread, mollified

• 1 egg

• 1 tablespoon apricot jam

• 6 tablespoons generally useful flour

• 1 tablespoon unsweetened cocoa powder

Directions

1. Slightly heat an air fryer to 320 degrees F. Splash a little fluted tube dish with cooking shower.

2. Beat sugar and spread together in a bowl utilizing an electric blender until light and smooth. Include egg and jam; blend until joined. Filter in flour, cocoa powder, and salt; blend all together. Empty player into the readied dish. Level the outside of the hitter with the rear of a spoon.

3. Place dish in the air fryer bushel. Cook until a toothpick embedded into the focal point of the cake turns out neatly, around 1about five minutes.

Spaghetti in Poblano Salsa

Ingredients

3 poblano chiles

¼ cup (25g) hacked white onion

2 garlic cloves, stripped

¼ cup (13g) new level leaf parsley

1 cup (240ml) entire milk

½ cup (120ml) Mexican crema

1 tablespoon salted spread

1 pound (455g) bucatini pasta

2 inlet leaves

Ocean salt and newly ground dark pepper

Disintegrated cotija cheddar and olive oil, to embellish

CHAPTER SEVEN

VEGETABLE RECIPES

Broiled Rainbow Vegetables in the Air Fryer

Ingredients

• 1 red chile pepper

• 1 yellow summer squash

- 1 zucchini

- 4 ounces new mushrooms, cleaned and divided

- 1/3 sweet onion

- 1 tablespoon extra-virgin olive oil

- Salt and pepper, add to taste.

Directions

1. Slightly heat an air fryer as per maker's proposals.

2. Place red chime pepper, summer squash, zucchini, mushrooms, and onion in an enormous bow. Include olive oil, salt, and dark pepper and hurl to join.

3. Put the vegetables in layers in the air fryer bushel. Air-fry vegetables until simmered, around 20 minutes, blending part of the way through cooking time.

Air-Fryer Roasted Veggies

Ingredients

• 1/2 cup diced zucchini

• 1/2 cup diced summer squash

• 1/2 cup diced mushrooms

• 1/2 cup diced cauliflower

• 1/2 cup diced asparagus

• 1/2 cup diced sweet red pepper

• 2 teaspoons vegetable oil

• 1/4 teaspoon salt

• 1/4 teaspoon ground dark pepper

• 1/4 teaspoon wanted flavoring (thoughts underneath), or more to taste

Directions

1. Slightly heat the air fryer to about 360 degrees F.

2. Add vegetables, salt, pepper, oil, and wanted flavoring to a bowl. Hurl to cover; organize in fryer crate.

3. Cook vegetables for 10 minutes, mixing the following about five minutes.

Note:

If utilizing firm vegetables (new potato, carrot, turnip, parsnip, winter squash, celeriac, sweet potato), cook for1about five minutes, mixing at regular intervals.

Nourishment

Per Serving: 37 calories; 2.4 g fat; 3.4 g starches; 1.4 g protein; 0 mg cholesterol; 152 mg sodium.

Fried Artichoke Hearts

Ingredients

• Artichoke hearts – canned, jolted (in water, not oil), or solidified.

• Breading – panko, preparing powder, bread pieces, parmesan, and flour

• Egg, only 1

• Flavor crew – salt, Italian flavoring

• Olive oil for splashing (I utilized a Misto)

Notes

• This is one handful of air fryer plans where it is critical to Slightly heat your air fryer. There's nothing more needed than 2 minutes, so don't skirt this progression.

• You can leave the artichoke hearts entire or cut them down the middle. I did a blend, and they cooked the two different ways uniformly. I discovered them simpler to eat when divided.

• If you have to make your breaded artichoke hearts without dairy, supplant the parmesan cheddar with 2 tsp of wholesome yeast.

• Have issues with eggs? Utilize your preferred veggie-lover mayo as the folio for the flour and breadcrumbs.

• If utilizing bumped artichoke hearts, ensure you get the ones stuffed in water and not oil. The oil will keep the breading from staying admirably.

• If utilizing solidified artichokes, there is no compelling reason to defrost them first.

Fried Artichoke Hearts!

Ingredients

• 1 can artichoke hearts, depleted (15 oz)

• 1/4 cup panko

• 1/4 cup bread morsels (prepared or unseasoned)

• 1/4 cup universally handy flour

• 2 tbsp ground Parmesan cheddar

• 1/2 tsp heating powder

• 1/4 tsp fit salt

• 2 tsp Italian flavoring (dried)

• 1 egg (beaten)

2 tsp olive oil

Instructions

1. Drain the artichoke hearts and press any extra water out of them.

2. In one bowl, consolidate bread morsels, panko, Italian flavoring, parmesan cheddar, and salt and blend well. Blend flour and heating powder in another bowl. Blend an egg in a third bowl. Set up a vacant plate.

3. It least demanding to work in clusters of 2-3. With your left hand, dig three artichoke hearts through the flour and shake the abundance off.

4. Then, drop them into the egg blend, mixing to cover.

5. Use your correct hand and drop them into the breadcrumb bowl. Spot your completed artichokes onto the plate.

6. Heat the air fryer to about 380 degrees F.

7. I suggest splashing the artichoke hearts with olive oil shower while they're still on the plate. Truly coat them.

8. Spray the crate of the air fryer with olive oil and tenderly spot the artichoke hearts in the bin. Try not to pack the container.

9. Cook them for about five minutes at 380 degrees F. Flip (most straightforward to utilize the tines of a fork). Splash the tops with extra olive oil shower if they need it.

10. Cook for an extra 3 minutes and afterward present with your most loved plunging sauce.

Oven Instructions

1. Follow stages 1-5 above.

2. Place material on a rimmed heating sheet, and spot a preparing rack on the sheet. Splash the rack generously with olive oil.

3. Place the artichoke hearts on the preparing rack and splash them generously with olive oil.

4. Then, bake at 425 degrees F for 2about five minutes, flipping partially through.

Air Fryer Asparagus

Ingredients

• 1 pound asparagus wooden closures cut

• 1 tsp olive oil

• pinch fit salt discretionary

Instructions

1. Slightly heat air fryer to 400 degrees F.

2. Remove the woody closures from the stalks.

3. Add asparagus to the bin of your air fryer. Daintily spritz/shower with olive oil.

4. Cook for at least seven minutes until they have arrived at your ideal degree of freshness.

5. Sprinkle completed asparagus with a touch of ocean salt. Serve right away.

Try not to be forceful with spritzing the olive oil on the stalks. A lot of olive oil = soft asparagus.

Nourishment

Calories 32 Calories from Fat 9

% Daily Value

Fat 1g2%

Soaked Fat 0g0%

Cholesterol 0mg0%

Sodium 2mg0%

Potassium 229mg7%

Starches 4g1%

Fiber 2g8%

Sugar 2g2%

Protein 2g4%

Nutrient A 7%

Nutrient C 6.4mg8%

Calcium 27mg3%

Iron 2.4mg13%

Percent Daily Values depend on a 2000 calorie diet.

Potatoes Firm Ranch Air Fryer

You'll locate a point by point and printable formula card at the base of this post.

Slice your potatoes to the ideal size. I like to utilize red potatoes, and I don't strip them. It makes this dish simpler to prepare, they're more beneficial, and that skin crisps up like a fantasy.

Notes

• Serve scraps with some Make-Ahead Scrambled Eggs for a wonderful breakfast skillet. Need to include some meat? Take a stab at heating bacon in the oven or this Whole30 Breakfast Sausage.

• If you'd like the potatoes to cook quicker, cut the pieces little; nearly diced. Check the following 10 minutes after cooking.

• Prepare a cluster while you have everything out of the zest cabinet.

• If you'd prefer to utilize crisp garlic rather than garlic powder, include it at the midway cooking point to keep away from it consuming. You may likewise adore utilizing Air Fryer Roasted Garlic for an all the more smooth garlic season.

• You can cook the spuds early as a feature of your simple solid dinner prep. To warm, pop them again into the air fryer for about five minutes at 400 degrees F.

Broiled Ranch Air Fryer Potatoes

Ingredients

- 1 lb potatoes (skin on)

- 1 tsp olive oil

- 1/2 tsp chives (dried)

- 1/2 tsp parsley (dried)

- 1/4 tsp dill (dried)

- 1/2 tsp garlic powder

- 1/4 tsp onion powder

- 1/2 tsp legitimate salt

- 1/8 tsp dark pepper

- 1/8 tsp celery seed

- 1/2 tsp tarragon (dried)

Instructions

1. Cut your potatoes to the ideal size. There is no compelling reason to strip them except if you lean toward that.

2. Add up the olive oil, potatoes, and seasonings in a blending bowl, hurling to cover.

3. Heat the air fryer to about 380 degrees F for three minutes.

4. Spray within the air fryer with olive oil and include potatoes. Cook for 1about five minutes and afterward shake the bushel to blend the potatoes around.

5. Cook for an extra 10-1about five minutes or until they have arrived at your ideal degree of fresh.

Nourishment

To warm, cook in the air fryer for about five minutes at 400 degrees F.

Firm Ranch Air Fryer Potatoes

Fat 1g2%

Soaked Fat 1g6%

Sodium 180mg8%

Potassium 468mg13%

Starches 15g5%

Fiber 3g13%

Sugar 1g1%

Protein 3g6%

Nutrient C 13mg16%

Calcium 37mg4%

Iron 4mg22%

Percent Daily Values depend on a 2000 calorie diet.

Notes

• Every individual lean towards their veggies simmered to a particular level. Utilize sound judgment and keep an eye on your Brussels during the cooking procedure to perceive what works best for you.

• Yes, you can make these early! Store in an air-tight compartment and microwave for 30 seconds. Simply don't be the a-gap who takes them to work and smells up the lunchroom kitchen.

• (oven technique). Make sure the oven is completely Slightly heating up before you include the sprouts. The high warmth assists with crisping them up without making them saturated.

• (oven technique). Don't stuff the container with an excessive number of Brussels as it will make them steam as opposed to caramelizing and simmering. Utilize a subsequent container if you have to cook a ton.

• (oven strategy). You'll need to cook these Brussels grows on the base rack of the oven to help burn these little folks into sweet, simmered obscurity.

Varieties

• Try the flavoring from these Spicy Sweet Potato Fries to kick up the wow factor on these air fryer Brussels grows.

• Throw in some firm bacon for a smoky and heavenly flavor. You can include uncooked bacon with the remainder of the ingredients and cook alongside the sprouts. Or then again simply include some cooked bacon toward the end for crunchy little nibbles of meat candy.

• Toss completed sprouts with a squirt of new lemon squeeze and top with Parmesan cheddar.

• Hit the completed Brussels with a sprinkle of balsamic.

This simple side dish of Air Fryer Brussels Sprouts is so flavorful and sound. Firm and caramelized because of the oven or air fryer.

Ingredients

• 2 cups Brussels grows (cut down the middle, quartered for huge sprouts)

• 1 tbsp olive oil

• 1/4 tsp ocean salt

Air Fryer Brussels Sprouts Method

1. Slightly heat air fryer to 375 degrees F for about five minutes.

2. Lightly shower the crate with olive oil cooking splash. Include the sprouts and cook for 9 minutes or to your ideal degree of fresh.

3. Salt completed sprouts to taste.

Oven Roasting Instructions

1. Slightly heat the oven to 450 degrees and spot a rack in the most reduced setting.

2. Combine Brussels, the salt, olive oil, and garlic cloves in a bowl. Hurl to cover.

3. Dump the bowl onto a rimmed heating sheet and spread the veggies around to give them space. Presently, be annoyingly fastidious and ensure they are completely chopped side down on the dish. Irritating, yet this is going to give you the ideal singe!

4. Bake for 12 minutes. Mix and heat for another 3-8 minutes relying upon your ideal degree of fresh.

Notes

Ensure the oven is completely Slightly heating up before you include the sprouts. The high warmth assists with crisping them up without making them spongy. Cook on the base rack.

Try not to pack the bushel (air fryer strategy) or container (oven technique) with an excessive number of Brussels as it will make them steam as opposed to caramelizing and cooking. Utilize a subsequent dish if you have to cook a great deal.

Each inclines toward their veggies cooked to a particular level. Utilize good judgment and mind your Brussels during the cooking procedure to perceive what works best for you.

Sustenance Facts

Sum Per Serving (0.75 cups)

Calories 50 Calories from Fat 36

% Daily Value

Fat 4g6%

Immersed Fat 1g6%

Sodium 156mg7%

Potassium 171mg5%

Sugars 4g1%

Fiber 2g8%

Sugar 1g1%

Protein 1g2%

Nutrient A 332IU7%

Nutrient C 37mg45%

Calcium 18mg2%

Iron 1mg6%

Percent Daily Values depend on a 2000 calorie diet.

Air Fryer Cauliflower - Is Roasted Cauliflower Healthy?

Hell truly, it is! What's more, I am additionally attracting a line the sand and saying simmered cauliflower is more delectable than crude, steamed, or some other planning. Come to me.

At the point when you place veggies with a dash of oil in a hot oven, otherworldly things occur. The sugars in the vegetables caramelize, and the dish will become better and all the more fulfilling. Also, gnawing into a superbly simmered veggie is such a great amount of better than attempting to eat one that is limp, boring, and overcooked.

Why You Should Use an Air Fryer

Air Fryers are magnificent little ledge convection ovens that can impersonate the taste and surface of fried foods with practically zero oil. I have this Power XL fryer and have been content with it.

Air Fryers are somewhat not the same as a convection toaster oven in that they flow the air through the little "fry" container.

The outcome is the firm "fried" food that isn't oily or overwhelming.

One of the greatest selling focuses for the air fryer, as I would see it, is that you get prepared/fried foods without expecting to utilize your oven. In the mid-year, it's dazzling not to warm up your entire house since you have a craving for some prepared cauliflower.

For this formula, the air fryer will deliver superbly broiled cauliflower in less than 20 minutes. It will take in any event 30 minutes in the oven to get a similar degree of firm prepared cauliflower.

Air Fryer Cauliflower Ingredients

• Cauliflower

• Olive oil

• Kosher Salt

• Potato Starch (discretionary)

Notes

• Do not add salt to the cauliflower until it is finished cooking in the air fryer. Pre-salting the veg will make it discharge overabundance dampness, bringing about soft veggies.

• No air fryer? Prepare on a sheet dish in an oven Slightly heat up to 425 degrees. Cook for 18 minutes, mix and meal until it has arrived at your ideal degree of fresh (generally 5-1about five minutes longer).

Light, tasty, and firm Air Fryer Cauliflower is the ideal side for quick smart dieting. Top with your preferred flavors or sauce for a simple formula.

Ingredients

• 16 oz cauliflower cut into florets

• 1 tbsp potato starch

• 1 tsp olive oil

• Salt and pepper to taste

Instructions

1. Set your air fryer to about 380 degrees F and then slightly heat up for about three minutes.

2. Cut your cauliflower into uniform pieces. In the case of utilizing potato starch, hurl with the florets in a profound blending bowl. Sprinkle in the olive oil and mix to cover.

3. Lightly splash within the fry bin with olive oil cooking shower and include the cauliflower.

4. Cook for 8 minutes, shake the crate, and cook for an extra 5-10 minutes relying upon your ideal degree of "fresh."

5. Sprinkle simmered cauliflower with new parsley, fit salt, and your seasonings or sauce of decision.

Notes

Try not to have any or need this to be keto-accommodating? Simply forget about it.

Try not to add salt to the cauliflower until it is finished cooking in the air fryer. Pre-salting the veg will make it discharge abundance dampness, bringing about soft veggies.

No air fryer? Heat on a sheet skillet in an oven Slightly heat up to 425 degrees. Broil for 18 minutes, mix and dish until it has arrived at your ideal degree of fresh (normally 5-1about five minutes longer).

Nourishment

Fat 1g2%

Soaked Fat 0g0%

Cholesterol 0mg0%

Sodium 28mg1%

Potassium 287mg8%

Starches 5g2%

Fibre 1g4%

Sugar 1g1%

Protein 1g2%

Nutrient C 43.7mg53%

Calcium 20mg2%

Iron 0.4mg2%

CHAPTER EIGHT

POULTRY RECIPES

Sound chicken bosom (oven toaster)

Ingredients

• 1 huge chicken bosom

• Soy sauce

- Sesame oil

- Honey

- Garlic powder

- Salt

- Pepper

- Oregano

- Any cooking oil

Steps

1. Marinate chicken bosom in soy sauce, sesame oil, and nectar for at least 60 minutes.

2. Create a compartment utilizing foil and coat within a region with cooking oil

3. Place the chicken bosom on the aluminum foil and season with salt, pepper, garlic powder, and oregano. Warmth it in the oven toaster for 7-8 mins. Flip it a while later and cook for another 7-8 mins or until within is cooked.

Breaded Parmesan Chicken w/Mozzarella Pan Pasta (Toaster Oven)

Ingredients

- 2 cuts chicken bosoms with no skin

- 1/2 cup breadcrumbs

- 3 tbsp parmesan cheddar

- 1 egg beaten

- 1 squeeze paprika

- cooking oil

- cooked pasta

- 50 grams of tomato glue

- Three cloves garlic

• 2 little tomatoes hacked

• To taste salt and pepper.

• 5 tbsp mozzarella destroyed

Steps

1. Mix the breadcrumbs, Parmesan, paprika, salt, and pepper. In a different bowl, beat up egg.

2. Season the chicken with salt and pepper.

3. Insert the chicken in the egg and then coat with the breadcrumb blend. Put aside to dry

4. Fry the chicken in medium warmth. Put aside when cooked on kitchen paper to deplete the overabundance oil.

5. In a sauce container, saute garlic and tomatoes. Pour in the tomato glue and the pasta. Include 2 tbsp of parmesan and season to taste.

6. Pour in the pasta in the toaster oven container and top in the breaded chicken. Put cuts/destroyed mozzarella on top and heat in the oven until mozzarella is liquefied.

Rotisserie Chicken Parmesan Crunchwrap

Ingredients

• 1 cup destroyed rotisserie chicken

• 1/4 cup Mexican or cheddar mix

• 1 huge burrito wrap

• 1 crunchy tostada

• 3 tablespoons Sarayo (2 sections mayo, 1 section siracha)

• 1 teaspoon parmesan cheddar

Steps

1. Shred your rotisserie chicken into a bowl and combine it with the Sarayo to make a zesty chicken serving of mixed greens.

2. Heat enormous burrito wrap on a stovetop skillet. Spot tostada in the center and include your cheddar, and a fiery chicken plate of mixed greens overtop being certain not to go over the tostada.

3. Make the folds by collapsing up one side and making nonstop overlap in one direction, beginning close to the center of the past crease until you have shut the wrap.

4. Grill on the stovetop to seal in the base or put in an oven or toaster oven for 10 minutes to seal the base overlays together.

Tricia's Chicken Zucchini Boats

Ingredients

• Two zucchini cuts the long way

• 1 oz destroyed carrots

• 1 oz hacked onion

• 1 oz cut child Bella mushrooms

• 8 oz boneless skinless chicken bosom

- 4 oz goat cheddar disintegrates

- 1 tsp Olive Oil

- 12 new basil leaves

- 1/2 tsp onion powder

- 1/2 tsp garlic powder

- 1/2 tsp Himalayan salt

Steps

1. Slightly heat the oven to 425 or cook in the toaster oven on 450

2. Slice zucchini the long way, scoop the meat out of the center and put in a safe spot

3. Line zucchini vessels in a goulash dish, splash with Olive Oil, season with a touch of salt, garlic

4. Place zucchini vessels in the oven for 20 minutes

5. Heat a skillet over medium warmth and include oil, chicken, garlic, carrots, onions, mushrooms and seasonings

6. Saute until chicken and vegetables are seared and delicate

7. Remove vessels from oven and fill.

8. Top with goat cheddar and new basil

9. Cook and extra 10 to 1about five minutes

Shrimp meatball in tomato basil sauce

Ingredients

• 10 shrimps

• Minced chicken

• Scallion

• Garlic

• 1 tbsp potato starch

- Salt

- Pepper

- 1 tbsp olive oil

- Tomato basil sauce

- Ketchup

- Mustard

- 1-2 leaves inlet leaf

- 1 tbsp cooking wine

Steps

1. Follow "pre-treatment of shrimp."

2. Mix minced scallion, minced chicken, potato starch, salt, and pepper.

3. Wrap No.2 on each shrimp and make into meatballs

4. Add garlic and olive oil on a fry-container, cook until softly caramelized surface shows up on both side

5. Add tomato basil sauce, ketchup, mustard, sound leaf, cooking wine, salt, and pepper and cook in low warmth for 5-10min

6. Take out and place on heat-verification dish-products. Sprinkle some cheddar and warmth for 3min in oven-toaster. At that point, sprinkle some dry herbs.

Simple Baked Chicken

• You need around 4 ounces of chicken bosom (evacuate the skin),

• ¼ teaspoon of thyme,

• ¼ teaspoon of oregano,

• ¼ teaspoon of rosemary, naturally ground dark pepper, salt, and a tablespoon of olive oil.

Direction

1. Line the over toaster skillet with aluminum foil.

2. Place equivalent measures of flavors on the two sides of the chicken bosom.

3. Place chicken on the aluminum foil-lined skillet and pour olive oil over the chicken.

4. Bake is putting the toaster oven on a "heat" setting for around 3about five minutes in 350 degrees Fahrenheit.

Heated Chicken Recipe

This is another variety of heated chicken; however, to make chicken increasingly delightful, the meat is marinated in advance.

You need a bit of chicken bosom or an entire chicken thigh marinated for around four hours in buttermilk or soy sauce, garlic, pepper, and narrows leaves.

Direction

1. Slightly heat your toaster oven to about 340 degrees Fahrenheit or utilize the "heat" setting on the oven.

2. You may cover the chicken with corn supper, salt, and pepper, paprika, and garlic, or you may utilize breadcrumbs prepared with flavors.

3. Place aluminum foil over the toaster oven plate and afterward shower oil or sprinkle olive oil.

4. Place the covered or non-covered chicken on the plate, sprinkle more oil over the chicken to abstain from drying the meat.

5. Bake for around 4about five minutes until the meat is finished.

Cooked Chicken with Lemon and Sage

• You will require two boneless and skinless chicken bosoms cut into equal parts,

• 3 tablespoons of olive oil,

• 2 tablespoons of crisp lemon juice,

• 2 tablespoons of crisp sage leave hacked into little pieces, a little clove of garlic minced,

• ½ teaspoon of ground lemon pizzazz,

• ¼ teaspoon of ground dark pepper and a scramble of salt.

Direction

1. Flatten boneless chicken with a hammer and afterward put in a safe spot. In a blending bowl, consolidate oil, sage leaves, lemon pizzazz, lemon squeeze, pepper, and salt.

2. Place the chicken in the blend and afterward place in a resealable sack to marinate for around 6 hours or medium-term.

3. Heat the toaster oven by putting it in sear. Add ¼ cup of water to the trickle plate of the toaster oven; place the chicken on the searing skillet, and afterward cook through for around 1about five minutes.

4. Turn the chicken and afterward keep cooking for an additional 1about five minutes. Serve your lemon and sage chicken embellished with crisp lemon cuts and sage leaves.

Broiled Chicken with Herbs

• You need around 7 ounces of chicken strips, a tablespoon of olive oil,

• ½ tablespoon of herbs,

• 2 tablespoons of Dijon mustard,

• A tablespoon of nectar, salt, and newly ground dark pepper.

Direction

1. Prepare your toaster oven by warming it to 450 degrees. Spot the toaster oven plate in and shower with olive oil—season chicken with salt, pepper, and herbs.

2. Place the chicken pieces on the plate and afterward shower with olive oil on top to abstain from drying.

3. Bake the chicken pieces for around 8 to 10 minutes; check the meat and keep cooking until it is cooked through.

4. Prepare the nectar and mustard blend.

5. Serve the chicken together with the nectar mustard sauce as an afterthought.

Chicken Sandwich

• This is produced using extra chicken, tomato, mozzarella cheddar, basil, and entire grain bread.

• Shred or drop extra chicken and afterward put in a safe spot.

• Place tomato, cheddar, basil, and chipped chicken in the middle of two cuts of entire grain bread.

Direction

1. Heat your Breville toaster oven to around 250 degrees Fahrenheit

2. Place chicken sandwiches in the toaster oven plate and afterward toast until the cheddar pieces are softened.

3. Cut the sandwich into two preceding you serve.

4. You may likewise attempt a bread-less form by putting cubed or cleaved remaining chicken in the sticks.

5. Put sticks on chicken alongside cherry tomatoes, red peppers, and corn. Prepare this for around 15 to 20 minutes in your toaster oven.

CHAPTER NINE

PORK RECIPES

Cajun Pork Chops - Exact Heat Toaster Oven

These oven-heated hacks have a brilliant dark colored covering. Present with garlic pureed potatoes and a green plate of mixed greens for a fast supper.

Ingredients

Vegetable oil cooking shower

1½ teaspoons garlic powder

1½ teaspoons paprika

1 teaspoon cayenne pepper

1 teaspoon salt

1 teaspoon dried thyme

½ teaspoon finely ground white pepper

¼ teaspoon finely ground dark pepper

1/3 cup wheat germ

¼ cup plain bread scraps

½ cup decreased fat milk

1 huge egg

4 boneless focus cut midsection cleaves, around 6 ounces each

2/3 cup generally useful flour

Healthful data

Healthful data per serving: Calories 681 (49% from fat) • carb. 24g • professional. 63g • fat 37g • sat. Fat 14g • chol. 204mg • turf. 643mg • calc. 18mg • fiber 0g

Instructions

1. Spot Cuisinart® Exact Heat™ Toaster Oven Broiler rack in position B and Slightly heat the oven to 375°F on the Bake setting. Spot searing container in the trickle plate in the lower position. Daintily cover the searing container with vegetable oil cooking splash and add ¼ cup water to the dribble plate.

2. Consolidate garlic powder and the next 6 ingredients in a little bowl (through dark pepper). Partition flavor blend down the middle and save each in a level container, (for example, a pie plate).

3. Include wheat germ and bread scraps to one of the level dishes and tenderly join.

4. Consolidate milk and egg in a medium bowl until all-around mixed.

5. Spot flour in a third level container. Dig every pork hack in the plain flavor blend. At that point, the flour, milk blend, and wheat germ blend.

6. Organize pork hacks in a solitary layer on the readied dish. Heat for 20 minutes; turn and prepare until juices are clear and meat is never again pink, around 20 minutes longer (inside temperature of pork ought to be 165°F). The exterior of pork hacks ought to be brilliant, dark-colored.

Crisp Herb-Crusted Pork Roast

Ingredients

3 garlic cloves, stripped

2 tablespoons crisp oregano leaves

2 tablespoons crisp rosemary leaves

2 tablespoons crisp thyme leaves

1 tablespoon Dijon-style mustard

1 teaspoon crisp lemon juice

1/4 teaspoons genuine salt

1/4 teaspoon crisply ground dark pepper

1 3-pound pork flank, (recently brined whenever wanted)

Nourishing data

Nourishing data per serving (4 oz):

Calories 229 (58% from fat) • carb. 1g • sugars 5g • professional. 22g • fat 14g • sat. fat 5g

• chol. 71mg • turf. 309mg • calc. 31mg • fiber 0g

Instructions

1. Put the garlic, oregano, rosemary, and thyme into the cleaving cup. Select Speed 5 and heartbeat to hack, around 8 to multiple times generally. Include mustard, lemon squeeze, salt, and pepper—a procedure to join ingredients, around 20 seconds completely.

2. Rub pork flank with herb glue. Slightly heat the oven to 425° F. (Permit pork to sit at room temperature while the oven warms up.)

3. Cook pork until the inward temperature arrives at 145°F, around 40 minutes. If you incline toward all around done, cook until the inside temperature arrives at 155°F.

4. Permit pork to rest for at any rate 10 minutes before cutting.

5. Utilizing the blade connection on speed, cut the pork into even cuts by keeping your hand consistent and applying medium strain to the meat in a descending movement.

Pulled Pork

Ingredients

Dry Barbecue Rub:

¼ cup stuffed light darker sugar

3 tablespoons bean stew powder

2 teaspoons Cajun flavoring

1 teaspoon smoked paprika

1 teaspoon genuine salt

1 teaspoon crisply ground dark pepper

5 to 6 pounds entire pork shoulder (bone-in)

Grill Sauce:

1 teaspoon olive oil

1 medium onion, stripped and cut

6 garlic cloves, stripped and finely cleaved

1 teaspoon Worcestershire sauce

1 cup chicken stock, diminished sodium

½ cup bean stew sauce, (for example, Heinz)

¼ cup juice vinegar

¼ cup molasses

2 tablespoons tomato glue

1 tablespoon light dark colored sugar

1 teaspoon moment coffee powder

Healthful data

Healthful data per serving

(In light of 12 servings):

Calories 521 (61% from fat) • carb. 17g • genius. 33g

• Fat 35g • sat. Fat 12g • Chol. 134mg • grass. 855mg

• Calc. 56mg • fiber 1g

Instructions

1. Combine the focus on ingredients in a little bowl. Rub everywhere throughout the pork shoulder and permit to marinate in an enormous preparing dish or a 2-gallon resealable sack in the cooler medium-term.

2. After the pork has marinated, put the oil in the cooking pot of the Multicooker set to Brown/Sauté at 400°F. When the unit has Slightly heated up, dark-colored the pork well on all sides, around 3 to 4 minutes for each side. Evacuate furthermore, hold.

3. Lessen warmth to 350°F and include the onion and garlic; sauté until relaxed, around 3 to about five minutes.

4. While the onion and garlic are cooking, blend the remainder of the ingredients in a little bowl until joined. When the vegetables have softened, mix in the sauce.

5. Heat sauce to the point of boiling and add the pork back to pot; go to cover in sauce and spread, change the unit to Slow Cook on Low for 12 hours.

6. To serve, shred pork straightforwardly in the pot, either with tongs or gloved hands, into reduced down pieces. Evacuate bones and dispose of them. Shred meat well into the sauce to join.

CHAPTER TEN

BEEF RECIPES

Each air fryer and brand is made diversely, and the occasions underneath probably won't work for your air fryer. It will be ideal if you check the instructions manual that accompanies your air fryer. The greater part of them nowadays have instructions and a manual for pass by for cooking meat.

Speedy temperature control for cooking steak:

Uncommon 120

Medium Rare 125

Medium 135

Medium Rare 140 to 145

Would I be able to cook a solidified steak in my air fryer?

I have not tried this formula utilizing a solidified steak, and I could never, at any point, cook a steak from solidified in the air fryer. If your steak is solidified, let it defrost in the ice chest medium-term or let it sit out for two or three hours with the goal that it comes to room temperature.

Step by step instructions to make Air Fryer Steak:

1. In a nonstick skillet, cook the ground meat on medium-high warmth. At the point when the meat is dark-colored and never again pink in the center, channel any additional fat. Include onion powder, garlic powder, and Worcestershire sauce. Put in a safe spot.

2. Dice the pickles, tomatoes, and onions.

3. Add 2 cups of hacked romaine lettuce, pickles, tomatoes, onions, cheddar, and ground hamburger to the highest point of the lettuce.

4. Top the plate of mixed greens with two tablespoons of Thousand Island dressing.

Tips for Air Fryer Steak:

Various types of Steak Temps, Time, Minutes

Filet Mignon – 8 oz 400 degrees 18 min

London Broil – 2 lb 400 degrees 20 to 28 min

Rib Eye, bone-in (1 in) – 8oz 400 degrees 10 to 15 min

Sirloin Steaks – (1 in) 12 oz – 400 degrees 9 to 14 min

What is an Air Fryer?

This is a kitchen apparatus, and it cooks by flowing sight-seeing around the food utilizing the convection system. It is a scaled-down variant of the convection oven.

Is air fried food solid?

At the point when you contrast air fried food with pan-fried food, it is a lot more beneficial because there is not any oil utilized whatsoever. The main oil I use is from my Pam cooking shower. I splash just the food on more than one occasion because most air fryer bushels are non-stick. If you are worried about utilizing vaporized showers for nature or your wellbeing purchase, a Misto Brushed Aluminum Oil Sprayer can from Amazon and fill that with your preferred oil.

What are the Best Large Size Air Fryers?

If you are inquiring about air fryers and hoping to purchase the best ones out there available, I have attempted and tried two distinct ones preceding. If you need to have the option to prepare more food for your family without a moment's delay at that point, get an air fryer with an enormous bin, for example, 5.3 quarts. Search for ones that state nonstick on them and have numerous program settings.

Ingredients

• 2 – 12 oz New York Strip Steaks (1in thick)

• Salt and Pepper to taste two tablespoons of spread (discretionary)

Instructions

1. If your air fryer requires Slightly heat uping, Slightly heat your air fryer.

2. Set the temperature to 400 degrees Fahrenheit.

3. Season your steak with salt and pepper on each side.

4. Place the steak in your air fryer bin. Try not to cover the steaks. Set the opportunity to 12 minutes and flip the steak at 6. Present with vegetables or squashed cauliflower. This will give you a medium uncommon steak.

Notes

Steak time can be very contingent upon what size it is.

Air Fryer Steak Recipe

Ingredients

• 1 New York Strip Steak or Ribeye Steak

• Kosher Salt (to taste)

• Black Pepper (to taste)

• Garlic Powder (to taste)

• Paprika (to taste)

• Butter

Instructions

1. Allow meat to sit at room temperature—shower olive oil on the two sides of the steak.

2. Season meat with fit salt, dark pepper, garlic powder, and paprika.

3. Slightly heat air fryer to 400F.

4. Place steak in the air fryer and cook for 12 minutes. Flip partially through. This turns out to medium doneness.

5. Top with margarine.

Notes

Rest the steak for about eight minutes before cutting.

Air Fryer Roast Beef

Ingredients

- 2 lb hamburger broil top round, or eye of round is ideal

- Oil for splashing

Rub

- 1 tbs legitimate salt

- 1 tsp dark pepper

- 2 tsp garlic powder

- 1 tsp summer savory OR thyme

Instructions

1. Mix all rub ingredients and rub them into broil.

2. Place fat side down in the bushel of the air fryer (or set up for rotisserie if your air fryer is so prepared)

3. Lightly splash with oil.

4. Set fryer to 400 degrees F and air fry for 20 minutes; turn fat-side up and splash softly with oil. Keep cooking for 15 extra minutes at 400 degrees F.

5. Remove the dish from the fryer, tent with foil, and let the meat rest for 10 minutes.

6. The time given should deliver an uncommon meal, which ought to be 125 degrees F on a meat thermometer. Extra time will be required for medium, medium-well, and well. Continuously utilize a meat thermometer to test the temperature.

7. Approximate occasions for medium and well separately are 40 minutes and 4about five minutes. Make sure to utilize a meat thermometer as times are rough consistently, and fryers contrast by wattage.

Nourishment

Serving: 1g | Calories: 238kcal | Carbohydrates: 1g | Protein: 25g | Fat: 14g | Saturated Fat: 6g | Cholesterol: 89mg | Sodium: 1102mg | Potassium: 448mg | Vitamin A: 55IU | Vitamin C: 0.3mg | Calcium: 37mg | Iron: 3mg

Air Fryer Steak

Steak sizes will fluctuate long, and thickness and various cuts will cook at various rates, so you can include or diminish cooking time if necessary to cook to your favored surface.

Ingredients

• 2 (6 oz.) steaks, 3/4" thick flushed and tapped dry

• 1 teaspoon olive oil, to cover

• 1/2 teaspoon garlic powder (discretionary)

• Salt, to taste

• pepper, to taste

• Butter

Directions

1. Lightly coat steaks with olive oil. Season the two sides of steaks with garlic powder (discretionary), salt, and pepper (we'll ordinarily season generously with salt and pepper).

2. Slightly heat the Air Fryer at 400°F for 4 minutes.

3. Air Fry for 400°F for 10-18 minutes, flipping midway, however (cooking time reliant on how thick and cold the steaks are in addition to how do you incline toward your steaks).

4. If you need steaks to be cooked more, include extra 3-6 minutes of cooking time.

5. Add a pat of spread on steak, spread with thwart, and permit steak to rest for about five minutes.

6. Season with extra pepper and salt to taste. Serve right away.

Air Fryer Steak Bites with Mushrooms (or without)

We had a little steak in the cooler and considered making a pan-fried food out of it. That is somewhat our go-to dinner. Something basic with a little protein and a few veggies is our dependable, fast, and simple weeknight burger joint. At that point, we contemplated the air fryer and needed to cook something else. Presto! Air fryer steak nibbles rung a bell and OMG, and it was the best dinner choice ever. These steak nibbles are pleasantly scorched outwardly and flawlessly cooked within. It knocked our socks off how basic and magnificently cooked the steak chomps were.

We have three diverse air fryers, every single, distinctive brand, and we unquestionably have our top picks.

• Size matters, particularly in case you're expecting to take care of a group of four to six hungry individuals.

• We're generally cooking for two during the bustling weeknights, and the three qt size fryers are incredible for us.

• If you're thinking about what size of air fryer to get, our suggestion is the 3-4 qt sizes for 2-3 individuals (or if it's all the same to you cooking numerous clusters) and the 5-6 qt for groups of 4-6 (you'll despite everything cook somethings in bunches, yet not as much as the littler air fryers).

Air Fryer Steak Bites and Mushrooms

We cooked the steak in a 3.4 qt. Air Fryer. Bigger Air Fryers may cook quicker. A few brands of Air Fryers will cook slower or quicker than others, modify in like manner.

For the kinds of steak, utilize your top pick. Contingent upon the financial limit, we incline toward ribeye, sirloin, tri-tip, and toss shoulder steaks (otherwise known as London Broil steaks).

Ingredients

• 1 lb. steaks, cut into 1/2" 3D shapes (ribeye, sirloin, tri-tip or what you like)

• 8 oz. mushrooms (cleaned, washed and split)

• 2 Tablespoons Butter, liquefied (or olive oil)

• 1 teaspoon Worcestershire sauce

• 1/2 teaspoon garlic powder, discretionary

• flaky salt, to taste

• Fresh broke dark pepper, to taste.

• Minced parsley, embellish

• Melted spread for completing - discretionary.

• Chili Flakes, for completing - discretionary.

Directions

1. Rinse and altogether pat dry the steak shapes. Join the steak solid shapes and mushrooms. Coat with the liquefied spread and afterward season with Worcestershire sauce, discretionary garlic powder, and a liberal flavoring of salt and pepper.

2. Slightly heat the Air Fryer at 400°F for 4 minutes.

3. Spread the steak and mushrooms in an even layer in the air fryer bushel. Air fry at 400°F for 10-18 minutes, shaking and flipping and the steak and mushrooms multiple times through cooking process (time relies upon your favored doneness, the thickness of the steak, size of air fryer).

4. Check the steak to perceive how all around done it is cooked. If you need the steak increasingly done, include an additional 2-about five minutes of cooking time.

We are topping with parsley and shower with discretionary softened spread and additionally discretionary bean stew pieces. Season it with extra pepper and salt whenever wanted. Serve warm.

Air Fryer Steak Tips Recipe

Because of the high warmth and a decent fan that courses the warmth uniformly all around the food, you get firm outside without overcooking within. In this way, the Air fryer resembles a profound fryer without huge amounts of oil and oil, or like the super grill that cooks the foods equally all around.

Hamburger Steak Tips

Making the meat steak tips in the air fryer rather than some other strategy (oven, oven, flame broil, cast iron skillet) has a few advantages. My preferred one is the negligible cleanup. If you somehow happened to cook the steak tips in a cast iron, you have to turn on your stove fan since things will get smoky. Also, everything around the skillet inside 2 feet will be shrouded in a layer of oil splatter.

With the air fryer, everything is contained inside the shut bushel of the air fryer. So you, despite everything, get all the incredible steak nibble flavors (singing/sautéing and all) sans the oil shower.

If you somehow managed to utilize the oven, it is difficult to get the steak tips seared without overcooking within, and the cooking is the place the flavor is concentrated.

251

Simple Air Fryer Recipe

Steak tips Marinade Ingredients

• Spices: I utilize my preferred handcrafted blend of flavors for the marinade, yet if you have your preferred zest blend, you're free to utilize that as well.

• Steak Choice: This formula utilizes ribeye steak, however the new york strip or some other slice is OK to use also.

Step by step instructions to cook the Steak tips

• Slightly heat the air fryer for about five minutes.

• Season the steak tips meat with flavors and hurl to cover well.

• Spread the steak nibbles along the base of the frier and cook on one side. At that point, go to the opposite side and include asparagus.

Tips for progress for steak nibbles:

• Do not stuff the air fryer container when cooking. The more space you have between every steak chomp, the more sight-seeing is ready to circle, which makes a pleasant outside all around.

• You can – pre-marinade the meat. If you do, don't include salt until directly before cooking it.

• Make sure you trim all of the connective tissue or huge bits of fat from the meat.

Ingredients

• 1.5 lb steak or hamburger hurl for a less expensive rendition slice to 3/4 inch blocks

Air Fryer Steak Marinade

• 1 tsp oil

• 1/4 tsp salt

• 1/2 tsp dark pepper, crisply ground

• 1/2 tsp dried garlic powder

- 1/2 tsp dried onion powder

- 1 tsp Montreal Steak Seasoning

- 1/8 tsp cayenne pepper

Air Fryer Asparagus

- 1 lb Asparagus, intense closures cut (could supplant with lances of zucchini)

- 1/4 tsp salt

- 1/2 tsp oil (discretionary)

Instructions

1. Slightly heat the air fryer at 400F for around about five minutes.

2. Trim the steak off the fats and cut it into 3D squares. At that point, hurl with the ingredients for the marinade (oil, salt, dark pepper, Montreal flavoring, onion, and garlic powder and the

cayenne pepper) and back rub the flavors into the meat to cover equitably. Do this in a ziplock pack for simpler cleanup.

3. Spray the base of the air fryer crate with a nonstick shower if you have any and spread the readied meat along its base. Cook the hamburger steak tips for around 4-6 minutes and check for doneness.

4. Toss the asparagus with 2/3 tsp oil and 1/4 tsp salt until equitably covered.

5. Once the steak nibbles are sautéed exactly as you would prefer, hurl them around and move to the other side. Add all of the asparagus to the other side of the air fryer container and cook for an additional 3 minutes.

6. Remove the tips of the steak and the asparagus to a plate and then serve while hot.

Notes

It's sheltered to open the air fryer whenever to beware of the meat. Open the air fryer after around 4-about five minutes of cooking and verify whether it caramelized just as you would prefer, at that point cook further or turn the steak pieces and include the asparagus immediately, or keep cooking the steak chomps for a few minutes more.

Nourishment

% Daily Value

Fat 34g52%

Soaked Fat 14g88%

Cholesterol 138mg46%

Sodium 703mg31%

Potassium 913mg26%

Starches 6g2%

Fiber 3g13%

Sugar 2g2%

Protein 49g98%

Nutrient A 1210IU24%

Nutrient C 8.5mg10%

Calcium 52mg5%

Iron 7.1mg39%

Percent Daily Values depend on a 2000 calorie diet.

Awsome Air Fryer Steak

A splendidly burned steak can appear to be an overwhelming errand. Getting the brilliant, dried up burn outwardly and doing whatever it takes not to overcook your steak can be troublesome. Think of a scenario where your air fryer can remove the entirety of that pressure. It's valid! Leave it to the air fryer to cook an ideal bit of steak all without filling your kitchen with smoke or turning on the flame broil. Concerning the herb spread? It's not required. However, it sure is flavorful.

We picked a thick-cut ribeye here. However, if you lean toward an alternate cut of steak, you can, in any case, utilize the air fryer. Simply make certain to alter the ideal opportunity for a more slender cut.

Ingredients

4 tbsp. margarine, mellowed

2 cloves garlic, minced

2 tsp. naturally cleaved parsley

1 tsp. naturally cleaved chives

1 tsp. naturally cleaved thyme

1 tsp. naturally cleaved rosemary

1 (2 lb.) bone-in ribeye

Legitimate salt

Newly ground dark pepper

Directions

1. In a little bowl, consolidate spread and herbs. Spot in the focal point of a bit of cling wrap and fold into a log. Turn closes together to keep tight and refrigerate until solidified, 20 minutes.

2. Season steak on the two sides with salt and pepper.

3. Place steak in the crate of air fryer and cook at 400° for 12 to 14 minutes, for medium, contingent upon the thickness of the steak, flipping part of the way through.

4. Top steak with a cut of herb spread to serve.

Air Fryer Mongolian Beef

Ingredients

Meat

• 1 Lb Flank Steak

• 1/4 Cup of Corn Starch

Sauce

• 2 Tsp of Vegetable Oil

• 1/2 Tsp Ginger

- 1 Tbsp of Minced Garlic

- 1/2 Cup of Soy Sauce

- 1/2 Cup of Water

- 3/4 Cup of Brown Sugar

Additional items

- Cooked Rice

- Green Beans

- Green Onions

Instructions

1. Thinly cut the steak in long pieces, at that point cover with the corn starch.

2. Place in the Airfryer and cook on 380 for about five minutes on each side. (Note - in light of surveys, I have transformed it to about five minutes on each side. Start with about five minutes and increment if necessary.)

3. While the steak concocts, warm up all sauce ingredients in a medium estimated pan on medium-high warmth.

4. Whisk the ingredients together until it finds a good pace bubble.

5. Once both of the steak and sauce are cooked together, ensure to place the steak in a bowl with the sauce and let it absorb for around 5-10 minutes.

6. When prepared to serve, use tongs to evacuate the steak and let the overabundance sauce dribble off.

7. Add the steak on cooked rice and green beans, top with extra sauce if you like.

Notes

Recall that all air fryers will in general warmth in an unexpected way, I recommend checking the steak after around about five minutes, to be certain it finds workable pace doneness.

The most effective method to Cook Steak in an Air Fryer

Not all air fryers are made equivalent, so make a point to peruse the instruction manual for your specific model before cooking.

For this test, I utilized the Power Air Fryer XL. To keep things decent and straightforward, I chose a New York strip steak, which is lean, delicate, and delightful when cooked appropriately. Here are the specific ingredient breakdown and technique I followed:

- 1 9 ½ oz. New York strip steak

- ¼ tsp Kosher salt

- ¼ tsp newly ground dark pepper

- 1 tsp olive oil

Direction

1. Bring the steak to room temperature (this causes it to cook all the more equitably). Then, set the air fryer to about 380 degrees and pre-heat it for 3 minutes on any setting. While you're pausing, expel overabundance fat from the edges of your steak— it should pull off effectively. However, you can utilize a sharp blade.

2. Season the steak and rub it done with olive oil. Spot the steak inside the air fryer container, set the temperature to 400 degrees, and the cooking time for 7 minutes if you incline toward medium-uncommon.

3. Flip the steak part of the way through cooking, expel it from the air fryer, and let it rest for around 10 minutes before cutting.

The Power Airfryer XL has a steak preset. However, I simply don't suggest utilizing it. This setting—which changes the temperature to 400 degrees and cooks time to 12 minutes—is just valuable in case you're cooking a bigger cut of hamburger like a bone-in ribeye. For littler cuts like strip steak, 12 minutes of cooking is excessively long.

CHAPTER ELEVEN

SEAFOOD RECIPE

Air Fryer Fish

Ingredients

1 lb. cod, cut into four strips

Fit salt

Naturally ground dark pepper.

1/2 c. universally handy flour

1 enormous egg, beaten

2 c. panko bread morsels

1 tsp.

Old Bay flavoring

Lemon wedges, for serving.

Tartar sauce for serving.

Directions

1. Pat fish dry and season on the two sides with salt and pepper.

2. Place flour, egg, and panko in three shallow dishes. Add Old Bay to panko and hurl to join. Working each, in turn, coat fish in flour, at that point in egg, lastly in panko, squeezing to cover.

3. Working in clusters, place fish in a container of air fryer and cook at 400° for 10 to 12 minutes, tenderly flipping part of the way through, or until fish is brilliant and pieces effectively with a fork.

4. Serve with lemon wedges and tartar sauce.

Firm Air Fryer Fish

Ingredients

Ingredients

- 4-6 Whiting Fish filets cut down the middle

- Oil to fog

Fish Seasoning

- ¾ cup exceptionally fine cornmeal

- ¼ cup flour

- 2 tsp old inlet

- 1 ½ tsp salt

- 1 tsp paprika

- ½ tsp garlic powder

- ½ tsp dark pepper

- OR

- Your most loved fish flavoring

Instructions

1. Combine ingredients for fish flavoring in a Ziplock sack and shake. Set to the side. In the other option, you could utilize your preferred fish flavoring.

2. Rinse and pat dry your fish filets with paper towels. They should, in any case, be clammy. Spot fish filets in ziplock pack and shake, until filets are completely secured with flavoring.

3. Place filets on a heating rack to permit any abundance flour to tumble off.

4. Grease the base of your air fryer container and spot the filets in the crate—Cook filets on 400 degrees for 10 minutes.

5. Open the crate and splash the fish as an afterthought that is looking up before flipping, guaranteeing that the fish is completely covered. Flip and cook the opposite side for 7 minutes. Evacuate fish and serve.

Notes

Adjust cook times if necessary, relying upon the thickness of the filet.

Air Fryer Garlic Shrimp

Simple Shrimp in Air Fryer

Continuously crisp and brimming with the season, this air fryer shrimp formula is incredible! Truly, this brief air-fried shrimp is too simple to even think about passing up. If you love shrimp as we do, it's anything but difficult to need to make this a few times each week. The air-fried shrimp turns out delicate with a magnificent nibble—the garlic and lemon flavors sparkle. Serve the shrimp on a plate of mixed greens, tacos, quinoa, or with anything you need. It's so useful for ordinary and cooks in around 1about five minutes. This low carb shrimp is ideal for occupied weeknights when you need to assemble dinner speedy.

Sound Air Fryer Shrimp Recipe

This formula for air fryer shrimp is truly low carb and sound. For the air fryer, you barely need to utilize any oil. A smidgen of olive oil splash is all your requirement for fresh shrimp. Try not to cook it excessively long, or it can get dry. In any case, if you like your shrimp somewhat more delicious, at that point, sprinkle with somewhat more oil before you cook. This will enable the shrimp to be progressively soggy and less dry.

Shrimp comes in various sizes, so you'll need to modify cooking times apiece. You'll calculate the best time for your air fryer after you've cooked a cluster.

Food: Air Fryer, Seafood

Servings: 2 - 3 Servings

Calories: 228 kcal

Ingredients

• 1 pound crude shrimp, stripped de-veined,

• Vegetable oil or shower, to cover shrimp

• 1/4 teaspoon garlic powder

• Salt, to taste

• Black pepper, to taste

• Lemon wedges

• minced parsley and additionally bean stew drops (discretionary)

Directions

1. In a bowl, hurl the shrimp with the oil. Include garlic powder, salt, and pepper and hurl to cover the shrimp equitably.

2. Add shrimp to air fryer containers in a solitary layer.

3. Air fry at 400°F for around 10-14 minutes, delicately shaking and flipping midway, contingent upon the size of shrimp.

4. Transfer shrimp to the bowl, crush lemon squeeze on top. Sprinkle parsley or potentially bean stew chips and serve hot.

Air Fryer Tuna Patties

Ingredients

• 2 container of Tuna in water

• 2 teaspoons Dijon Mustard

• 1/2 cup Panko Bread Crumbs

- 1 tablespoon lemon juice

- 2 tablespoons hacked parsley

- 1 egg

- 3 tablespoons olive oil

- Tabasco sauce, salt, and pepper to taste

Instructions

1. Drain the majority of the fluid from the canned fish. Blend the fish, mustard, bread pieces, lemon juice, and parsley in a bowl. Add some Tabasco exactly as you would prefer

2. If the blend appears to be somewhat dry, include a tablespoon of olive oil and blend

3. Add the egg and join. Add salt and pepper to taste

4. On a sheet of heating, paper spoon the fish blend into patties.

5. To assistance keep the patties fit as a fiddle, refrigerate for an hour or two (or medium-term, if conceivable)

6. Slightly heat your air fryer to 360F

7. Place you're each of the patties in the air fryer and cook for about 10 minutes. If you need them to be extra fresh, leave the patties in for an additional 2 – about five minutes.

8. For extra firm, leave the patties in for an additional 2–about five minutes

9. Enjoy

Tilapia in your Air Fryer

Ingredients

• 3 Tilapia Filets

• 1 tablespoon Olive oil

• Your decision of flavoring to taste (discretionary)

Instructions

1. Slightly heat your air fryer to 400F

2. Brush the tilapia with the oil and giving a decent in any event, covering

3. Add the flavoring you've picked, sprinkle everywhere

4. Spritz the air fryer bin with non-stick cooking splash

5. Place the Tilapia in the air fryer bin

6. Set the air fryer time to eight minutes, then slide the bin in, and cook

7. Turn the fish midway however

8. Once the time is done, ensure to check the fish id it is cooked through (some air fryers may take as long as fifteen minutes)

9. Enjoy

Solid Air Fried Salmon

A basic yet delectable approach to appreciate a solid salmon dinner. You can make you possess flavor blend and simply utilize our instructions as a manual for how to cook salmon and make your own air fried salmon dinner. (Cooking settings for air singing solidified salmon will be extraordinary!)

Ingredients

• 500 grams of salmon

• 1/2 teaspoon garlic powder

• 1/2 teaspoon paprika

• 1/2 teaspoon legitimate salt

Instructions

1. Preheat the Air Fryer to 280F

2. Mix the flavors and salt, and disperse over the salmon.

3. Put the salmon, and skin side down in the bushel, and cook for 10 minutes. Alter the time, as indicated by your taste.

4. Remove and serve!

Mollusks Oreganata

Ingredients

• 1 cup unseasoned breadcrumbs

• 1/4 cup Parmesan cheddar, ground

• 1/4 cup parsley, hacked

• 1 teaspoon dried oregano

• 3 clove garlic, minced

• 4 tablespoons spread, softened

• 2 dozen mollusks, shucked

Instructions

1. 1. In a medium-sized bowl, consolidate the breadcrumbs, Parmesan, parsley, oregano, garlic, lemon pizzazz, and liquefied margarine. Blend to make morsels.

2. 2. Spot a piling tbsp of the morsel blend onto the uncovered shellfishes. Fill the Copper Chef cake embed with a cup of coarse

ocean salt. Settle the shellfishes in the salt and cook at 400 for 3 minutes—enhancement with new parsley and lemon wedges.

Air-Fryer Fish and Fries

Ingredients

• 1 pound potatoes (around 2 medium)

• 2 tablespoons olive oil

• 1/4 teaspoon pepper

• 1/4 teaspoon salt

• FISH:

• 1/3 cup generally useful flour

• 1/4 teaspoon pepper

• 1 huge egg

• 2 tablespoons water

- 2/3 cup squashed cornflakes

- 1 tablespoon ground Parmesan cheddar

- 1/8 teaspoon cayenne pepper

- 1/4 teaspoon salt

- 1 pound haddock or cod fillets

- Tartar sauce, discretionary

Directions

- Slightly heat air fryer to 400°. Strip and cut potatoes the long way into 1/2-in.- thick cuts; cut cuts into 1/2-in.- thick sticks.

- In a huge bowl, hurl potatoes with oil, pepper, and salt. Working in groups varying, place potatoes in a solitary layer in an air-fryer container; cook until simply delicate, 5-10 minutes toss potatoes in bushel to redistribute; keep on cooking until daintily sautéed and fresh, 5-10 minutes longer.

- Meanwhile, in a shallow bowl, blend flour and pepper. In a separate shallow bowl, then proceed to whisk the egg with water.

277

In a third bowl, hurl cornflakes with cheddar and cayenne. Sprinkle fish with salt; dunk into flour blend to cover the two sides; shake off overabundance. Plunge in egg blend, at that point in cornflake blend, tapping to help to cover follow.

• Remove fries from the container; keep warm. Spot fish in a solitary layer in fryer bushel. Cook until fish is gently seared and simply starting to drop effectively with a fork, turning partially through cooking, 8-10 minutes. Try not to overcook. Return fries to the bin to warm through. Serve right away. Whenever wanted, present with tartar sauce.

Test Kitchen tip

In our testing, we have discovered cook times change significantly between brands of air fryers. Subsequently, we have given more extensive than ordinary ranges on recommended cook times. Start checking at the first run through recorded and change varying.

Nourishment

312 calories, 9g fat (2g soaked fat), 85mg cholesterol, 503mg sodium, 35g starch (3g sugars, 1g fiber), 23g protein. Diabetic Exchanges: 3 lean meat, 2 starch, 2 fat.

One Basket Fish and Chips

Another advantageous option in contrast to the conventional British Friday night treat, fish sticks, and French fries. Each twofold serving should be possible in one basket, on one cooking setting too, making this an exceptionally basic weekday supper.

• Servings: 2

Ingredients

• 200 grams white fish filet (tilapia, cod, Pollack)

• 30 grams tortilla chips

• 1 egg

• 300 grams (red) potatoes

• 1 tablespoon vegetable oil

• 1 tablespoon lemon juice

Instructions

1. Slightly heat your air fryer to 350°F

2. Cut the fish into four equivalent pieces, and this guarantees they cook through and rub with the lemon squeeze, salt, and pepper. Let the fish rest for about five minutes

3. Using a food processor, blitz the tortilla chips into fine pieces. In the food processor and move the ground tortilla chips to a plate.

4. Whisk the egg in a bowl

5. Now, dunk each fish piece into the egg individually and roll the bits of fish through the ground tortilla chips with the goal that they are secured

6. Clean, then cut the potatoes into dainty strips

7. Soak the potato strips in water for 30 minutes

8. Drain them and pat dry, at that point cover them with oil

9. Insert a separator in the air fryer bin. Spot the potato strips on one side and the bits of fish on the other

10. Set the clock to 12 minutes and fry until brilliant dark colored

Air Fryer Lobster Tail

Ingredients

• Four lobster tails

• 2 tablespoons of liquefied margarine

• 1/2 teaspoon salt

• 1 teaspoon pepper

Instructions

1. Slightly heat your air fryer to 380F

2. Cut the lobster through the tail area, and I would utilize a decent pair of kitchen scissors

3. The shell can be sharp. Crush and pull spirit the shell

4. Brush your lobster tails with the liquefied margarine, salt, and pepper

Spot the rich lobster tails in the air fryer bin and air fry at 380F for 4 minutes. Include the staying liquefied spread, and air fry for 2 minutes

CPSIA information can be obtained
at www.ICGtesting.com
Printed in the USA
LVHW082044030221
678276LV00008B/266